MISSOURI
OKLAHOMA
LOUISIANA
Lake Texoma
HAGERMAN NWR
Sherman
CADDO NAT. GRASSLAND
Red River
Bowie
Cooke
Grayson
Fannin
Lamar
Delta
RAY ROBERTS LAKE SP
Denton
Collin
Hunt
Hopkins
Franklin
Titus
Morris
Cass
Camp
Rockwall
Rains
Wood
Upshur
Marion
Tarrant
Dallas
L. Tawakoni
Harrison
Kaufman
Arlington
Van Zandt
Smith
Gregg
Longview
Johnson
Cleburne
Ellis
Henderson
Tyler
Panola
Rusk
Navarro
RICHLAND CREEK WMA
Hill
Anderson
Cherokee
Shelby
Bosque
Freestone
Nacogdoches
SABINE NF
McLennan
Limestone
San Augustine
Toledo Bend Reservoir
Waco
Houston
Lufkin
Sabine
Leon
DAVY CROCKETT NF
Angelina
ANGELINA NF
Falls
Temple
Trinity
Sam Rayburn Reservoir
Robertson
Madison
Polk
Bell
Walker
Lake Livingston
Tyler
Milam
Brazos
Bryan
Huntsville
Jasper
Newton
Sabine R.
Brazos R.
SAM HOUSTON NF
San Jacinto
Grimes
Hardin
Burleson
Austin
Lee
Montgomery
Conroe
W. G. JONES SF
Orange
Washington
Waller
Beaumont
Bastrop
Austin
Liberty
Jefferson
Port Arthur
San Marcos
Fayette
Harris
Chambers
Houston
Baytown
SABINE WOODS (TEXAS ORNITHOLOGICAL SOCIETY PRESERVE)
ATTWATER PRAIRIE CHICKEN NWR
ANAHUAC NWR
Pasadena
Colorado
PALMETTO SP
Fort Bend
Galveston
Rollover Pass
Gonzales
Texas City
Galveston
Lavaca
Wharton
Brazoria
BRAZORIA NWR
DeWitt
Jackson
Bay City
Freeport
Victoria
Matagorda
Goliad
Port Lavaca
Calhoun
Bee
Beeville
Refugio
ARANSAS NWR
GOOSE ISLAND SP
San Patricio
Aransas
Corpus Christi
Nueces
MUSTANG ISLAND SP
Kingsville
PADRE ISLAND NATIONAL SEASHORE
Gulf of Mexico
South Padre Island
LAGUNA ATASCOSA NWR
Harlingen
Cameron
LOWER RIO GRANDE VALLEY NWR

American Birding Association

Field Guide to Birds of Texas

Mark W. Lockwood

PHOTOGRAPHS BY
Brian E. Small
AND OTHERS

Scott & Nix, Inc.
NEW YORK

A SCOTT & NIX EDITION

PUBLISHED BY SCOTT & NIX, INC.
150 W 28TH ST, STE 1900
NEW YORK, NY 10001
SCOTTANDNIX.COM

FIRST EDITION 2016

THIRD PRINITNG 2021

ISBN 978-1-935622-53-6

AMERICAN BIRDING ASSOCIATION, INC.
800-850-2473
ABA.ORG

SCOTT & NIX, INC. BOOKS
ARE DISTRIBUTED TO THE TRADE BY:

INDEPENDENT PUBLISHERS GROUP (IPG)
814 NORTH FRANKLIN STREET
CHICAGO, IL 60610
800-888-4741
IPGBOOK.COM

FSC
www.fsc.org
MIX
Paper from
responsible sources
FSC® C119703

THIS BOOK IS PRINTED ON FSC® CERTIFIED PAPERS,
WHICH ASSURES IT WAS MADE FROM WELL MANAGED
FORESTS AND OTHER CONTROLLED SOURCES.

PRINTED IN SOUTH KOREA

Contents

The American Birding Association inspires all people to enjoy and protect wild birds.

The ABA represents the North American birding community and supports birders through publications, conferences, workshops, events, partnerships, and networks.

The ABA's education programs promote birding skills, ornithological knowledge, and the development of and implementation of a conservation ethic.

The ABA encourages birders to apply their skills to help conserve birds and their habitats, and we represent the interests of birders in planning and legislative arenas.

We welcome all birders as members.

THE AMERICAN BIRDING ASSOCIATION CODE OF ETHICS

Everyone who enjoys birds and birding must always respect wildlife, its environment, and the rights of others. In any conflict of interest between birds and birders, the welfare of the birds and their environment comes first.

CODE OF BIRDING ETHICS

1. Promote the welfare of birds and their environment.

    1(a) Support the protection of important bird habitat.

    1(b) To avoid stressing birds or exposing them to danger, exercise restraint and caution during observation, photography, sound recording, or filming.

Limit the use of recordings and other methods of attracting birds, and never use such methods in heavily birded areas, or for attracting any species that is Threatened, Endangered, or of Special Concern, or is rare in your local area; Keep well back from nests and nesting colonies, roosts, display areas, and important feeding sites. In such sensitive areas, if there is a need for extended observation, photography, filming, or recording, try to use a blind or hide, and take advantage of natural cover.

Use artificial light sparingly for filming or photography, especially for close-ups.

1(c) Before advertising the presence of a rare bird, evaluate the potential for disturbance to the bird, its surroundings, and other people in the area, and proceed only if access can be controlled, disturbance minimized, and permission has been obtained from private land-owners. The sites of rare nesting birds should be divulged only to the proper conservation authorities.

1(d) Stay on roads, trails, and paths where they exist; otherwise keep habitat disturbance to a minimum.

2. Respect the law, and the rights of others.

2(a) Do not enter private property without the owner's explicit permission.

2(b) Follow all laws, rules, and regulations governing use of roads and public areas, both at home and abroad.

2(c) Practice common courtesy in contacts with other people. Your exemplary behavior will generate goodwill with birders and non-birders alike.

3. Ensure that feeders, nest structures, and other artificial bird environments are safe.

3(a) Keep dispensers, water, and food clean, and free of decay or disease. It is important to feed birds continually during harsh weather.

3(b) Maintain and clean nest structures regularly.

3(c) If you are attracting birds to an area, ensure the birds are not exposed to predation from cats and other domestic animals, or dangers posed by artificial hazards.

4. Group birding, whether organized or impromptu, requires special care.

Each individual in the group, in addition to the obligations spelled out in Items 1 and 2, has responsibilities as a Group Member.

4(a) Respect the interests, rights, and skills of fellow birders, as well as people participating in other legitimate outdoor activities. Freely share your knowledge and experience, except where code 1(c) applies. Be especially helpful to beginning birders.

4(b) If you witness unethical birding behavior, assess the situation, and intervene if you think it prudent. When interceding, inform the person(s) of the inappropriate action, and attempt, within reason, to have it stopped. If the behavior continues, document it, and notify appropriate individuals or organizations.

Group Leader Responsibilities [amateur and professional trips and tours].

4(c) Be an exemplary ethical role model for the group. Teach through word and example.

4(d) Keep groups to a size that limits impact on the environment, and does not interfere with others using the same area.

4(e) Ensure everyone in the group knows of and practices this code.

4(f) Learn and inform the group of any special circumstances applicable to the areas being visited (e.g. no tape recorders allowed).

4(g) Acknowledge that professional tour companies bear a special responsibility to place the welfare of birds and the benefits of public knowledge ahead of the company's commercial interests. Ideally, leaders should keep track of tour sightings, document unusual occurrences, and submit records to appropriate organizations.

Everyone who enjoys birds and birding must always respect wildlife, its environment, and the rights of others. The ABA Code of Ethics should be read, followed, and shared by all birders.

Please follow this code and distribute and teach it to others.

The American Birding Association's Code of Birding Ethics may be freely reproduced for distribution/dissemination. An electronic version may be found at aba.org.

Foreword

Texans are known for bragging on their beloved Lone Star State but even many of Texas' biggest boosters aren't aware just how great their homeland is for birding. From Lesser Prairie-Chickens in the High Plains to Roseate Spoonbills along the Gulf of Mexico to Green Jays in the Lower Rio Grande Valley to Rufous Hummingbirds in the Trans-Pecos, Texas covers a lot of ground, both geographically and ornithologically. Texas birders are a wonderful, varied bunch, too, but one thing they almost never are is bored. Suffice it to say that if you've taken an interest in birding in Texas, you've really lucked out.

Like all the guides in this series, this book can help you do whatever you want with birding. Perhaps you enjoy birds a few days a year in your yard or local park and just want to know a little more about them and to know some of their names. Or maybe you want to dive deeper and really get familiar with the hundreds of amazing birds that call Texas home for part or all of each year. Our aim is to meet you where you are and give you useful, reliable information and insight into birds and birding.

You won't find a better guide to the birds here than Texas' own Mark Lockwood. His knowledge is formidable but he presents things in such a way that it illuminates rather than intimidates. The gorgeous photography by Brian E. Small and others will not only to aid your identifications—it will inspire you to get out and see more of these beautiful and fascinating creatures for yourself.

I invite you to visit the American Birding Association website (aba.org), where you'll find a wealth of free resources and ways to connect with the birding community that will also help you get the most from your birding in Texas and beyond. Please consider becoming an ABA member yourself—one of the best parts of birding is joining a community of fun, passionate people.

Now get on out there! Enjoy this book. Enjoy Texas. And most of all, enjoy birding!

Good birding,

Jeffrey A. Gordon

Jeffrey A. Gordon, *President*
American Birding Association

Birds in Texas

Texas is a very ecologically diverse state that is ideally located with a southern latitude and central longitude allowing a great diversity of bird life. Its central location makes Texas one of those states where the birds of both the eastern and western continent may be found. From east to west Texas is more than 800 miles across, which means that the bird life of the pine forests along the Louisiana border have very little in common with that of the Chihuahuan desert in the far west. Another important factor that adds to the birding possibilities in Texas is the Central Flyway. It brings a wide variety of birds through Texas that nest in Canada and the northern United States. In the eastern third of Texas, this is augmented by the Mississippi Flyway, which brings in more birds from farther east making woodland habitats along the immediate coast a great birding destination especially in spring. The western third of the state is part of the Central Flyway as well, but the vast majority of the migrants passing through there breed in the Rocky Mountains and west-central Canada.

The only place on earth that the Golden-cheeked Warbler nests is in oak-juniper woodlands of the Hill Country and northward to the vicinity of Possum Kingdom Lake.

The state has many birding attractions that have made it a very popular destination. Woodland habitats along the coast are renowned as places to be during spring migration to observe birds as they reach land after flying across the Gulf of Mexico from the Yucatan Peninsula. The Lower Rio Grande Valley is a must-visit location for birders who are interested in seeing tropical birds that only occur in the United States there. The Hill Country is home to the Golden-cheeked Warbler that nests nowhere else on earth. All in all, there are great places to study birds in all areas of Texas.

There have been 640 species of birds documented within the state. The Texas Ornithological Society, through the Texas Bird Records Committee, maintains the list of accepted species for the state. With a little effort it is possible to see 300 or even 400 species in a given year. Of course, it is a lot easier to reach one of these goals with a trip or two to the coast.

Birds in this Guide

This book includes 300 species which occur in the state every year and are, in general, fairly common. A few of the species included here are considered specialties of a particular region of the state. For example, the Red-cockaded Woodpecker is restricted to the Pineywoods. Of the remaining 240 species on the state list that are not included in this book are 150 that are very rarely seen in a given year. Others inhabit the open ocean and, as such, are very rarely seen from land or are very local or are difficult to find. A full list of the species documented in Texas (as of 2014) is included on pages 310–315.

The 300 birds in this guide are presented in the current taxonomic order, with a few minor exceptions, set out by the *American Ornithologists' Union's Check-list of North American Birds*. This is the sequence that most field guides follow and is revised to some extent almost annually. The order of birds is not intuitive and takes some time to learn. For a long time the sequence of birds was very stable, but great advances have been made in the study of DNA during the last 20 years that allowed scientists to better understand the relationships among species of birds. As a result, dramatic changes in our understanding of birds continues to reveal unexpected discoveries. This is the reason that the first species listed in older field guides was a loon and now it is a duck.

The sequence that birds are presented in a field guide does not always make sense, however, there are a number of ways that will help narrow the search in a field guide. These basic rules of thumb include:

- Birds in the first half of the book belong to groups that are familiar to most people (ducks, hawks, gulls, hummingbirds, etc.).
- Large birds are in the first half of the book.
- Water birds are found in the first half of the book.
- Songbirds are found in the second half of the book.
- Among the songbirds, those with pointed bills come first followed by those that have thick bills.
- Brightly colored, intricately patterned birds are often in the last quarter of the book.

These truisms are just a guide that will help in learning the taxonomic order of birds. The best teacher is the regular use of your field guide.

How to use the Species Accounts

Each species account includes the common and scientific name of the bird. As with the sequence of species, these follow the *American Ornithologists' Union's Check-list of North American Birds*. There is a basic description of the area in the state where that species is most likely to be encountered, as well as its relative abundance. The terms used to describe the status and abundance are defined as follows:

PERMANENT RESIDENT Occurs throughout the year and implies a breeding population.

SUMMER RESIDENT Implies a breeding population.

WINTER RESIDENT Occurs regularly between December and February.

MIGRANT Occurs as a transient passing through the state in spring and/or fall (certain species may be migrants in some regions and residents in others).

ABUNDANT Present in such numbers and in general distribution that in its proper habitat, many may be found in a given day.

COMMON Always present and in such numbers that one may expect to find several in a day.

UNCOMMON Normally present in proper habitat, but one cannot be sure of finding one in a day.

RARE On the average, it occurs only a few times a year in a given area or not at all. It is always a surprise to see one.

VERY RARE Not expected, occurs with some regularly, although not on an annual basis.

The strikingly plumaged Red-headed Woodpecker is a locally common permanent resident in the Pineywoods of East Texas.

Ecological Regions of Texas

Texas is a very ecologically diverse state that is easily divided into natural or ecological regions. Each region is unique and heavily influences the ranges of many kinds of birds, including some that are restricted to a specific region. The highest average rainfall in Texas is on the eastern edge of the state with the climate becoming increasingly arid father west. This precipitation regime, along with changes in soils and geology, defines the vegetation that is found in each region. Average rainfall amount varies from a low of about eight inches in the El Paso area to a high of more than 50 inches per year in the southeastern corner of the state.

The Pineywoods area is the easternmost ecological region in the state. It is part of the larger Gulf Coast Plain and is nearly level with elevations through the entire region only varying about 200 feet. It is dominated by mixed pine-hardwood forests with three common pines: loblolly (*Pinus taeda*), shortleaf (*P. echinata*), and longleaf (*P. palustris*). Despite the name, not all of the forests in the region are dominated by pines. There are mixed hardwood forests in bottomlands along the rivers that traverse the region.

The Coastal Prairies include prairies and marshes that are found on nearly level ground and generally within 80 miles of the Gulf Coast. These prairies are widest from the Louisiana border southward to Baffin Bay just south of Corpus Christi. From there to the Rio Grande the region consists of a narrow strip bordering the Laguna Madre. The transition from the Coastal Prairies to the Pineywoods and Oaks and Prairies region is abrupt except along drainages where riparian corridors extend into the prairies. The region grades more evenly into the South Texas Brush Country. The natural vegetation of the Coastal Prairies is tallgrass prairie with some areas of oak savannah. However, many of these grasslands have been invaded by trees and shrubs such as the exotic Chinese tallow (*Triadica sebifera*) and the native honey mesquite (*Prosopis glandulosa*).

West of the Pineywoods a large area with belts of forest, savannah, and grassland that make up the Oaks and Prairies regions. This region includes the Post Oak Savannah, Blackland Prairies, and

Cross Timbers sub-regions. Most of the region is dominated by gently rolling wooded savannahs with post oak (*Quercus stellata*) and blackjack oak (*Q. marilandica*). The Blackland Prairies intermingles with the Post Oak Savannah and historically was an expansive tallgrass prairie, but now about 98 percent of the region is under cultivation or converted to pasturelands.

The South Texas Brush Country is an area of brushlands primarily found south of the Hill Country. The vegetation of this region is dominated by brushy species which include honey mesquite, live oak (*Quercus virginiana*), and several acacias (*Acacia* sp.). The Lower Rio Grande Valley is found at the southern tip of this region. Historically, the floodplain of the Rio Grande supported diverse hardwood woodlands but the construction of dams along the Rio Grande has ended the seasonal flooding that once maintained these woodlands. The lack of flooding has resulted in a general encroachment of brush species from the north. The Coastal Sand Shield is another sub-region which is an area of deep sands found south of Baffin Bay. The sand plain is stabilized by vegetation for the most part and is largely dominated by live oak mottes.

The Western Scrub-Jay is a common permanent resident in the Hill Country and Trans-Pecos.

The Hill Country, or more formally the Edwards Plateau, is located in the center of the state. The Balcones Escarpment separates this region from the South Texas Brush Country to the south and the Blackland Prairies to the east. This region is a limestone uplift that is dissected by numerous streams and rivers. Canyons and slopes in the region support Ashe Juniper-oak forests. The northern and western parts of the region are characterized by semi-open grasslands and shrublands.

The Rolling Plains are situated between the High Plains and the Oaks and Prairies region in the north-central part of the state. These plains are nearly level to rolling and are dominated by honey mesquite savannahs and prairie. The Rolling Plains are divided from the High Plains by the steep Caprock Escarpment. Many rivers and streams in this region have eroded into the escarpment to form canyons. The largest and best known is Palo Duro Canyon. The canyons or breaks of the Canadian River are also included in this region. The Rolling Plains and the Edwards Plateau are ecologically similar, but a distinct geological change defines the boundary.

The High Plains are bounded by the Caprock Escarpment and dissected by the Canadian River. These plains are nearly level

The Painted Bunting is often one of the most common breeding birds in brushy habitats of the southern Rolling Plains and Edwards Plateau.

with many shallow lakes or playas. The original vegetation of the High Plains consisted generally of mixed and shortgrass prairie. Today, about 60 percent of the High Plains is in agricultural production, much of which is used to produce row crops. The southern extension of the High Plains, south of the Canadian River, is known as the Llano Estacado. The area around Lubbock, including the surrounding counties, is known as the South Plains.

The Trans-Pecos of far west Texas includes the northern extension of the Chihuahuan Desert. There are many small mountain ranges within the region with the Davis, Chisos, and Guadalupe Mountains being the best known. Guadalupe Peak, at an elevation of 8,751 feet is the highest point in Texas. These mountains ranges support pine and oak-juniper forests with desert grasslands and desert scrub found at lower elevations. The Stockton Plateau is a transitional area between the Edwards Plateau and the Chihuahuan Desert. The dominant vegetation type is honey mesquite and redberry juniper (*Juniperus pinchotii*) savannah.

The Montezuma Quail is restricted to several mountains ranges in the Trans-Pecos and to a small area in the southwestern Hill Country.

The Parts of Birds

Each of the birds included in this book is illustrated with one to three photographs. These images were chosen to depict individuals that are typical of that species and many of them were taken in Texas. There are species that comprise many distinct populations, or subspecies, that differ in subtle ways. A specific effort was made to only include images of birds that are in plumages that occur within the described range in the book. There are a few species that are quite variable, such as the Dark-eyed Junco, and in those cases the most common plumages are included.

Birds are an incredibly variable group of organisms. There are some species where the male and female look essentially the same, others where the sexes are markedly different. There are also birds that have more than one color morph that is retained throughout their lives. The illustrations included in this guide are intended to depict these differences. A few general rules are followed:

- For those species where the male and female look alike, only one image is used.
- If there is more than one distinctive color morph, such as Snow Goose or Reddish Egret, there are images of the different plumage types.
- For sexually dimorphic species, the first image is usually that of a breeding plumaged adult male.
- Some species change dramatically in plumage as they mature to adulthood, such as Little Blue Heron.

The captions that accompany each photo are not intended to be a complete description, but to point out characteristics that are helpful in identifying that particular species. The hope is that the combination of text, illustrations, and captions will provide the information needed to identify these birds. It is important to keep in mind that there are somewhat technical terms used to describe the parts of the bird that are included in the text. Learning the meaning of these terms will greatly enhance the usefulness of those descriptions.

PARTS OF A DUCK
This male Northern Shoveler shows major parts of a duck on the water's surface.

PARTS OF A GULL
This adult Ring-billed Gull shares many aspects with other gulls.

PARTS OF A RAPTOR
This perched Harris's Hawk shares many aspectes with other raptors.

The characteristics of a flying raptor are easily seen on this Northern Harrier. Note the black color of the outer primaries and white rump.

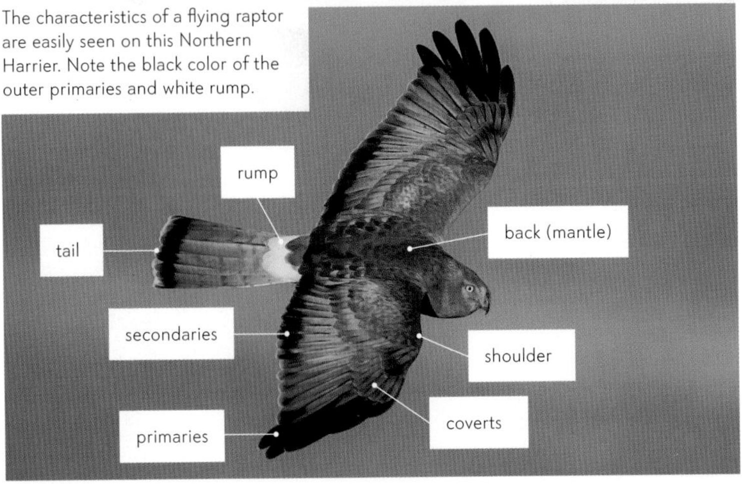

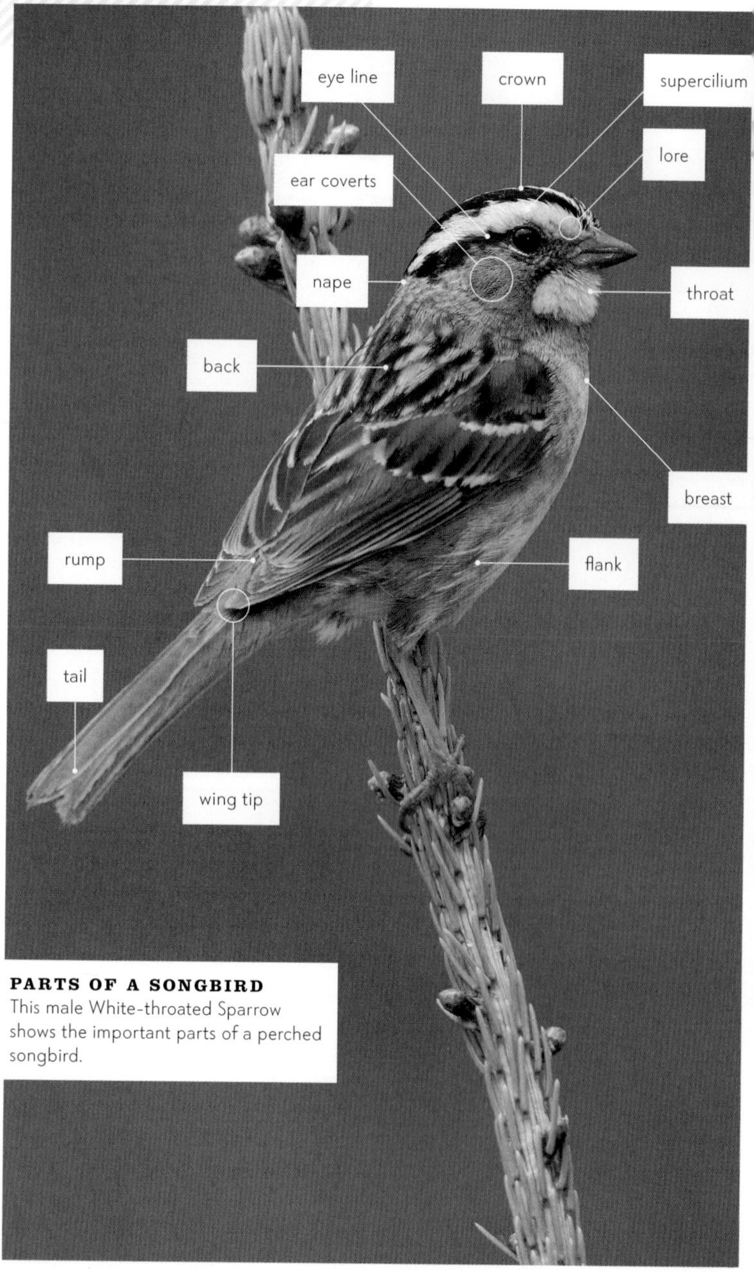

PARTS OF A SONGBIRD
This male White-throated Sparrow shows the important parts of a perched songbird.

The multilayered flight feathers of a female Mallard are revealed when she is aloft.

FLIGHT FEATHERS The long feathers of the wing are generally referred to as flight feathers and are divided into two groups. The longest of these feathers are the primaries and they form the tip of the wing. Depending on the group of birds there are either nine or ten. The inner group is referred to as the secondaries. These feathers are sometimes a different color, such as the speculum on some ducks.

The pale wing bars are clearly visible on this adult Northern Parula.

WING BAR An important identification clue in songbirds is often whether the bird has wing bars or not. The wing bar is formed by pale tips that form one or two lines across the folded wing.

The upper wing bar of the male breeding Western Tanager is bright yellow compared to the paler lower wing bar.

HEAD The head is often intricately marked and understanding these marks is very helpful in identification. Some terms are obvious, such as the top of the head being the crown. Others are not as clear and can vary among species. The following four images and captions point out a few of the more specialized descriptive terms used in identifcation.

Lighter feathers circling the eye are called the eye ring. The ring may extend into "spectacles" across the base of the bill, such as on this male Blue-headed Vireo.

The contrasting line above the eye is an eyebrow or supercillium. A dark line through the eye is generally referred to as an eye line, such as on this Eastern Meadowlark.

The area of feathers that covers the ears is called the ear coverts. These feathers can be differently colored from the remainder of the face, such as on this Clay-colored Sparrow.

The malar stripe is on the side of the throat and is usually dark. It is also called a whisker.

Identifying Birds

As with anything else, learning to identify birds takes practice. There are many birds that can be easily assigned to a well-known group, like a duck or a gull. There are also many birds that are easily identified simply through familiarity, such as a male Northern Cardinal. However, when observing an unfamiliar bird it is important to develop skills to help narrow down the possibilities. Making as assessment of the shape and size of the bird is always helpful. The shape of the bill is also a good feature to note. For songbirds noting if it has a thin, pointed bill for feeding primarily on insects or a heavy seed-eating bill makes it easier to narrow down to a particular group of birds. The structure of the wings and tail are also important. Does it have a long or short tail? On a perched bird how long are the wings when compared with the tail? These differences in structure can be as important as colors. Obviously noting color and pattern are also important. It is important to try not to rely on a single feature, but to look at the entire bird.

Warbling Vireos are rather nondescript birds, but can be identified by looking at the whole bird. The overall shape points to it being a perching bird and it has a narrow bill, supercilium, no wing bars, and medium-length tail. All of these features suggest that it is found in the second half of the book and in the first half of that section.

Additional Resources

Texas is a popular birding destination and as a result there is a plethora of information about the state's bird life. The primary source for status and distribution of the birds in Texas is the *TOS Handbook of Texas Birds*. It includes a detailed discussion of relative abundance, timing of occurrence, distribution (including a map for each species), and taxonomy but is not an identification aid.

The Texas Parks and Wildlife Department along with its partners have developed wildlife viewing trail maps. There are maps to all areas of the state and each map includes a large number of sites that are open to the public. Traditional bird finding guides for the state include two published by the *American Birding Association: A Birder's Guide to the Rio Grande Valley* includes the area from Brownsville to El Paso with sites throughout the Hill Country and Trans-Pecos and *A Birder's Guide to the Texas Coast*. These references should be consulted to get directions and full descriptions of birding locations.

There are two very popular field guides that cover all of the birds that occur in North American north of Mexico. *The National Geographic Field Guide to the Birds of North America* by Jon L. Dunn and Jonathan Alderfer and David Sibley's *The Sibley Guide to Birds* are both very well illustrated and have detailed accounts for each species. Both are outstanding and are highly recommended.

American Birding Association

Field Guide to Birds of Texas

Black-bellied Whistling-Duck

Dendrocygna autumnalis

L 18.5–20″ | **WS** 35.8″

Partially as a result of direct human actions, the population of Black-bellied Whistling-Ducks in Texas has grown exponentially since the mid-1980s. Prior to this population growth, these tropical ducks were basically a bird of South Texas. They are now common permanent residents throughout the coastal prairies and are found in varying densities as far north as the Dallas-Fort Worth area. Vagrants that may be the first colonizers have been found in all regions of the state. They use freshwater wetlands that can vary from natural habitats to agricultural areas and city parks. The rather nasal whistle these birds give makes it clear why the common name was changed from tree-duck to whistling-duck.

The long neck and legs separate this bird from most other waterfowl in Texas. The striking red bill of the adult is unique.

The broad white stripes are unmistakable when these birds are seen in flight.

Greater White-fronted Goose

Anser albifrons

L 25–31.8″ | **WS** 53.1

The vast majority of Greater White-fronted Geese that spend the winter in Texas are found on the coastal prairies, particularly between Houston and Corpus Christi. They are generally far outnumbered by Snow Geese that winter in the same area. These handsome geese are found in smaller numbers in the other areas of the state where Snow Geese spend the winter. There are two main wintering areas in North America; the coastal prairies of Texas and Louisiana and the Sacramento Valley in California. Migrants and winter residents are found between October and April.

The irregular black patches on the underparts give rise to the colloquial name "specklebelly."

Snow Goose

Anser caerulescens

L 27–33″ | **WS** 54″

The population of Snow Goose has seen a tremendous increase over the past two decades and as a result has become much more common in almost all areas in Texas. The largest concentrations are still found on the coastal prairies during winter where they mix with the very similar Ross's Goose (*Anser rossii*). The larger size and the black patch on the bill make the Snow Goose easy to distinguish from the smaller Ross's Goose. There are two color morphs that were once thought to be separate species with the dark birds called Blue Goose. White morph birds far outnumber dark morphs in Texas. Migrants and winter residents are found between October and mid-March.

The white morph of the Snow Goose is much more common in Texas. This is an adult with its immaculate white plumage; immature birds have varying amounts of gray.

The Blue Goose is distinctive with its white head contrasting with the blue and gray colors of the body. They also have the distinctive black "grin patch" on the bill like the white birds.

Canada Goose

Branta canadensis

L 29.9–43.3" | **WS** 50–67"

Although they can be found throughout the state, the northwestern portion of Texas is the primary winter area for the Canada Goose. This region is dotted with playas, small ponds that are filled by rain, which provide places for these geese to loaf during the day and roost at night. There are many subspecies of Canada Goose which vary considerably in size. The smallest of these are now considered to be a separate species, Cackling Goose (*Branta hutchinsii*). The Canada Goose has a distinctive, deep honking call where the Cackling Goose has a more nasal, higher pitched call. However, this can be hard to differentiate in a mixed flock. Migrants and winter residents are found between late October and early March.

These geese have rather long, thin necks and long bills giving then a sleeker look than the similar Cackling Goose.

Cackling Geese are smaller and have a more compact build than Canada Geese. The bill is much smaller and stubby, which is a good first point in identifying them.

Wood Duck

Aix sponsa

L 18.5–21.25" | **WS** 26–29"

A male Wood Duck is one of the most striking species of waterfowl in the world. These spectacular birds declined precipitously in the early 1900s, but have staged a significant comeback over the past fifty years. As a result, they are now a common sight in the eastern half of the state and are occurring with increasing frequency and abundance in the western half. Wood Ducks are most frequently encountered on forest ponds and other wetlands, but also use lakes in manicured city parks. They nest in cavities, sometimes well away from water. They readily use nest boxes and that has led to higher nesting rates and contributed strongly to the increase in abundance.

Adult males are unmistakable when they are in their full regalia. The prominent crest is iridescent purple and green which complements the reddish breast and yellow flanks.

Females are gray and brown. She also has a prominent crest and a tear-drop shaped ring surrounding the eye.

Gadwall

Mareca strepera

L 18.1–22.4″ | **WS** 33″

The Gadwall is a very common winter resident throughout the state. They are part of a large group of ducks that are frequently referred to as dabbling ducks. These birds feed primarily in shallow water by tipping down to reach food rather than diving. Although the plumage of the male Gadwall is dominated by gray and brown, the intricate patterning of the feathers makes them well worth a closer look. They are rare in the summer in the northwestern portion of the state with the bulk of the wintering population arriving during October and leaving in April.

The male's brown head contrasts strongly with the mostly gray body. The black bill and undertail separate it from other dabbling ducks with similar plumage patterns, such as a female Mallard.

The female has muted plumage that allows them to be camouflaged when incubating eggs. The grayish head contrasts with the browner body and the bill is mainly black with varying amounts of orange.

American Wigeon

Mareca americana

L 20" | **WS** 33"

The American Wigeon is one of the most common winter ducks and are often abundant on lakes and ponds, including in city parks. Unlike many other ducks, these birds are well-known for grazing well away from water and can be seen in agricultural fields and pastures. A colloquial name of this attractive duck is "baldpate" referring the unmarked white to tan crown of the male. Migrants and winter residents are found between October and March.

The broad green stripe the surrounds the eye and then extends back to the nape is an obvious field mark for these ducks. They have a short gray bill with a black tip that is quite different from the other dabbling ducks found in the state.

Females have many of the same plumage characteristics of the male, but lack the green on the head.

Mallard

Anas platyrhynchos

L 22″ | **WS** 34″

The male Mallard is one of the most familiar of all waterfowl. Although common winter residents, they are uncommon nesters with most breeding occurring in the Panhandle. Mallards found in the Trans-Pecos and southward along the Rio Grande belong to a separate population known as "Mexican Ducks." The more familiar migratory population generally arrives in September and early October and leaves in March. Domesticated Mallards are a common sight in city parks across the state, but they generally have lost the sleek look of the wild birds.

The bright green head and yellow bill of the male Mallard are unmistakable.

Females are brown overall with an orange and black bill.

Both the male and female "Mexican Duck" are similar to a female Mallard. The plumage is typically darker. Males have a bright yellow bill.

Mottled Duck

Anas fulvigula

L 17.3–24″ | **WS** 33.8″

Mottled Ducks are generally found only on the coastal prairies, although they have been known to wander well inland. They are fairly common in their range, although the population appears to be declining and conservation efforts are underway. Unlike many other species of ducks, Mottled Ducks tend to remain in pairs throughout the year and are not often found in mixed flocks with other ducks. Both sexes look very much like a female Mallard, but they have darker body plumage and the speculum is bordered with black rather than white.

The pale brown head contrasts strongly with the much darker brown body plumage. As in Mallards, the bill of the male is bright yellow and the female has an orange bill with varying amounts of black.

In flight, the blue speculum is bordered in black with very little to no white.

Blue-winged Teal

Spatula discors

L 15″ | **WS** 23″

The Blue-winged Teal is an abundant migrant throughout the state and an uncommon wintering bird mostly along the coastal prairies. These attractive ducks are an early sign of spring migration when the first ones start moving north in late February. The protracted spring migration means that a few are still around in early May. Since the males and females are very similar in plumage in the fall, the fact the they start passing through the state in late July carries much less fanfare.

The head of a male is blue-gray in color with a large white crescent across the face.

The females are nondescript overall and can be distinguished from the similar Green-winged Teal by the spotted undertail.

Cinnamon Teal

Spatula cyanoptera

L 14.1–16.9″ | **WS** 24.8″

The Cinnamon Teal is a bird of the western United States, and Texas is on the eastern edge of the range. As a result these birds are most common as migrants in the western half of the state. Even with that being the case, the wetlands of the coastal prairies provide excellent wintering habitat and this teal is often found throughout the coastal prairies. Although the male is unmistakable, the female is often difficult to separate from the closely related Blue-winged Teal. Fall migrants can be found as early as mid-August and winter birds usually are heading north before the middle of April.

In the spring, the rich cinnamon plumage of the male sets it apart from all other ducks, but in the fall they are often indistinguishable from the females.

As with many other ducks, the females are mottled brown. The longer, slightly flatter bill of the Cinnamon Teal helps distinguish it from a Blue-winged.

Northern Shoveler

Spatula clypeata

L 18″ | **WS** 30″

It does not take much imagination to determine how the Northern Shoveler got its name. The broad, spatulate bill is unique among the waterfowl of Texas. They strain water through baleen-like filaments to capture the very small organisms on which they feed. As a result, they are found on nutrient-rich water impoundments such as sewage treatment ponds. The bright green head of the male is reminiscent of a male Mallard, but the similarities end there. The bright white chest and reddish-brown flanks of the Northern Shoveler are obvious field marks. These birds are present from late September through May with a few non-breeding birds found in the summer.

A male Northern Shoveler is hard to misidentify with its unique bill and bright plumage.

As in the male, the female has a broad, flattened bill.

Northern Pintail

Anas acuta

L 20–30″ | **WS** 33–36″

The long, slender look of the male Northern Pintail separates it from all other dabbling ducks. The long, central tail feathers of a breeding-plumage male also are unique from all regularly occurring ducks in Texas. Northern Pintails are common winter residents throughout the state and are uncommon and rather local breeding birds in the northwestern reaches of Texas. They seem to prefer to nest in the vicinity of shallow ponds. Since this habitat is rather ephemeral, they are not as faithful to nesting sites as many other species of waterfowl. Migrants and wintering individuals can be found from September through April.

In breeding plumage, there is an iridescent strip of feathers starting at the eye and extending to the nape that is very similar to that of a male American Wigeon.

The female has a similar attenuated look of the male including long central tail feathers.

Green-winged Teal

Anas crecca

L 12.2–15.3″ | **WS** 20.4–23.2″

The Green-winged Teal is the smallest dabbling duck found in Texas. They are generally common migrants and winter residents in all areas of the state. These birds are found throughout the Northern Hemisphere, although some authorities consider the Eurasian form as a separate species. Although small numbers of Green-winged Teal have been found during the summer in Texas, there are only two known instances of nesting. Migrants and winter residents are found between September and April.

Males have rather ornate plumage and are readily identified by the chestnut head with a wide green stripe starting at the eye.

Adult females are mottled brown and tan, similar to many other dabbling ducks. Their small size and proportionally small bill helps with the identification.

Canvasback

Aythya valisineria

L 21" | **WS** 33"

The Canvasback is part of a group of diving ducks that are commonly referred to as "pochards." Since they dive to find food, these ducks are most often found in areas of deeper water. The profile of a Canvasback easily separates it from the similar plumaged Redhead. These birds are common migrants and winter residents throughout the state. The first birds reach Texas in mid-October and spring migrants start to leave as early as February.

The sloping forehead and large bill provide a distinctive profile. Adult males have a chestnut head and the black and white body plumage.

Females have the same overall appearance and plumage pattern as a male, but with brown and gray.

Redhead

Aythya americana

L 19″ | **WS** 29″

The Redhead is a common to abundant migrant and winter resident. In fact, the Laguna Madre is the most important wintering area in North America for this diving duck. They are found there by the tens of thousands feeding in the seagrass beds. Redheads can also be found on inland lakes, but they are generally rare to locally uncommon during the middle of winter in these areas. Migrants and winter residents can be found from October to March.

The chestnut-red head of the male is the obvious source for the common name. These birds have a very rounded head unlike the Canvasback.

Females look very much like a brown version of the male. They also have a very rounded head with a steep forehead.

Ring-necked Duck

Aythya collaris

L 17″ | **WS** 25″

Ring-necked Ducks are small diving ducks with a distinctive high forehead and angular head giving then an almost crested appearance. Only at close range and in good light can the chestnut neck ring referred to in the common name be seen. Ring-necked Ducks are common in winter on inland lakes throughout the state. They are similar in appearance to Lesser Scaup, but the dark back of the male and the obvious eye ring of the female are sure field marks. Migrants and winter residents can be found between October and February, but it is not uncommon for a few to remain through the spring into early June.

The black head of the male is highly iridescent and often looks purple in the right light. They have a grayish bill with an obvious white ring before the black tip.

Females have the same tricolored bill and peaked head of the male. They also have a narrow white eye ring that extends into a line behind the eye and a whitish patch at the base of the bill.

Lesser Scaup

Aythya affinis

L 17″ | **WS** 29″

The Lesser Scaup is probably the most familiar of the "pochards" that occur in Texas. They are common to abundant migrants and winter residents in virtually all areas of the state. The preferred wintering areas include inland lakes as well as along the coast in bays and estuaries. The upper Texas coast east through Louisiana is one of the important wintering areas for this species. Lesser Scaup can be found primarily between October and March.

The iridescent head of the male is slightly peaked at the crown and can look purplish or greenish depending on light conditions. The bill is gray overall with a small black tip.

Females are nearly entirely brown except for an obvious white patch on the face at the base of the bill.

Bufflehead

Bucephala albeola

L 14" | **WS** 21"

The striking black and white plumage of the male Bufflehead easily separates it from other ducks. They are also the smallest duck found in Texas and the puffball look of the round head gives them a unique look. Rather than being found in large flocks, they are generally alone or in small groups on their wintering grounds. Migrants and winter residents can be found between late September and early May.

The very round, fluffy looking head of the male is distinctive. Although the head generally looks black and white, under the right conditions the purple and green iridescence can be easily seen on the dark areas.

Females are grayish-brown overall with a very rounded head and a white cheek patch.

Hooded Merganser

Lophodytes cucullatus

L 17″ | **WS** 25″

Mergansers are true fish eaters with long serrated bills that help them capture their preferred prey. The male has a spectacular fan-shaped crest that is often raised. These birds are most often encountered in small groups and are often shy and quick to fly. Although largely silent, in the late winter and early spring the males will make a frog-like croaking sound. Hooded Mergansers are increasing in abundance in Texas and in the last twenty years have begun to nest in northeastern portion of the state. These nests have been found in boxes and on occasion these birds will lay their eggs in an active Wood Duck nest. Migrants and winter residents can be found between November and March.

Adult males are largely black above with a white chest and dull chestnut sides. The crest is white bordered with black and could only be confused with the male Bufflehead.

The female also has a rounded crest that can be held open, although this is a much rarer sight than in males.

Ruddy Duck

Oxyura jamaicensis

L 15″ | **WS** 23″

The Ruddy Duck belongs to a group of waterfowl known as "stiff-tailed" ducks. They have a rather long tail that is held down in the water when the birds are active and often cocked up when at rest. Males have a rufous-brown body in breeding plumage that gave rise to the common name, but they are most often seen in Texas in their gray winter plumage. Migrants and winter residents can be found between September and April.

In the winter, males are brownish-gray rather than ruddy. They do retain the blackish crown and prominent white cheek.

Just before migrating north in the spring, the males molt into the ruddy breeding plumage. At the height of breeding condition, the bill turns blue.

Females resemble winter males but have gray checks with a dark line through the middle.

Plain Chachalaca

Ortalis vetula

L 21.6″ | **WS** 25.9″

The Plain Chachalaca is part of a widespread tropical family of birds known as guans. The majority of their range is in Mexico and just reaches the United States in the subtropical thorn-scrub woodland of South Texas. They are a common sight in areas where this habitat is protected in the Lower Rio Grande Valley, such as Santa Ana National Wildlife Refuge or Bentsen-Rio Grande Valley State Park. These birds are partially arboreal and climb up in trees in the early morning to perform a loud, repeated chorus of *cha-cha-lac* that can be heard hundreds of yards away. Although Plain Chachalacas eat fruits and insects, they also will eat leaves.

The browns and olives of the plumage provide camouflage in the dense thorn-scrub woodland they inhabit.

Scaled Quail

Callipepla squamata

L 9.8–13.7″ | **WS** 14.9″

Scaled Quail is aptly named as most of the plumage on their body is edged with darker coloration giving them a very scaled look. Their blue-gray color and white crest have also earned them the colloquial names "blue quail" and "cottontop." These birds are found throughout much of the western half of the state, although they are all but gone from the western Hill Country. They can be found in open grassland as well as desert environments. The birds in the South Texas Brush Country are a different subspecies from elsewhere in the state and can be identified by a chestnut patch on the belly.

Males have intricately pattern body plumage with a white face and short crest. The mottled browns, blacks, and white of the plumage provide excellent camouflage. Both sexes have intricately patterned body plumage with a short crest.

Northern Bobwhite

Colinus virginianus

L 10″ | **WS** 12.9–14.9″

For the eastern half of Texas, the only species of quail present is the Northern Bobwhite. In recent decades, the populations of this bird have declined severely. The reasons for this decline are numerous, not the least of which in the abundance of nonnative fire ants, which attack emerging chicks, often as they hatch from their eggs. Northern Bobwhites are faring better in the Hill Country and Rolling Plains where conditions are too arid for these ants to thrive. These regions have also been less heavily impacted by urbanization and other changes in land-use that have been linked to the decline farther east. These birds are most often found in open grassland, although they do tolerate some woody vegetation. The male's distinctive whistled song, *bob, bob-white,* is always a treat to hear these days.

Males have intricately patterned body plumage with a white face and short crest. The mottled browns, blacks, and whites of the plumage provide excellent camouflage.

Females are very similar to males in appearance, differing most prominently by the buffy face.

Montezuma Quail

Cyrtonyx montezumae

L 7.8–9″ | **WS** 16.1–16.9″

The Montezuma Quail is one of the much sought after birds of the Southwest. Intricately marked, they are restricted to several mountains ranges in the Trans-Pecos and to a small area in the southwestern Hill Country. By far the most well-known place to see these birds in Texas is Davis Mountains State Park, although they are fairly common throughout that mountain range. Montezuma Quail need open woodland habitats with abundant tall grasses. They have very large feet with long claws that allow them to dig up the tubers of wood sorrels. Their habit of freezing when danger is near earned them the name "fool's quail" and they will often wait until the last minute before taking flight.

The spectacular harlequin mask of the male makes them a favorite among birders. Despite the striking plumage on the males face and underparts, their backs are mainly brown and black which allows them to be well hidden in the grass.

Females share the small crest on the back of the head, but are otherwise dressed in tans and browns.

Lesser Prairie-Chicken

Tympanuchus pallidicinctus

L 14.9–16.9" | **WS** 27"

In the 1800s, prairie-chickens were widespread in Texas with Greater Prairie-Chickens (*Tympanuchus cupido*) found in the prairies of east-central Texas and along the coast and Lesser Prairie-Chickens in the Panhandle southward through the High and Rolling Plains. By 2010, the Greater Prairie-Chicken was almost gone from the state, however, the Lesser Prairie-Chicken holds on in the eastern Panhandle and western South Plains. Conservation efforts are underway to try and protect the remaining populations of both species. Lesser Prairie-Chickens are found in grassland mixed with scrubby oaks and other shrubs on sandy soils. These birds have an intricate courtship behavior where males congregate in open areas called "leks" and display hoping to attract a female. The dominant males take the central areas of the lek and younger males are relegated to the outer edges.

One of the great spectacles of the bird life of Texas is the display of a prairie-chicken. The males inflate sacks on the sides of their neck as they stomp their feet and dance around in hope of attracting the attention of a female.

Females have much smaller tufts on the sides of the neck.

Wild Turkey

Meleagris gallopavo

L 42″ | **WS** 53″

The Wild Turkey is now a common and widespread species due to successful conservation programs. Changes to the landscape because of land-use in the first half of the twentieth century impacted the population and there were strong concerns that they would disappear from the entire eastern half of the state. Wild Turkey is by far the largest game bird in North America and they are found primarily in woodland and forest habitats. They typically roost in trees and can be easily disturbed at these roost sites.

The Wild Turkey is familiar to virtually everyone because of the widespread domestication of the species. The wild populations, however, have more intricately patterned plumage and are far more agile.

Females are considerably smaller than males with less iridescence to their feathers.

Common Loon

Gavia immer

L 31″ | **WS** 46″

The Common Loon is the only loon that is of common occurrence in Texas. These birds can sometimes be found in large concentration in protected bays. Even though the largest proportion of the wintering population is found there, they are also present on inland lakes as well, quite commonly on the large reservoirs in the eastern half of the state. Fall migrants arrive primarily in October and most have left the state for their breeding grounds by early April. Many that remain into the summer never molt out of non-breeding plumage, but a few will molt into breeding plumage and migrate.

Common Loons can be identified by their large size and the dagger shaped bill. They often swim low in the water so that the white of the underparts are not visible except on the breast.

Least Grebe

Tachybaptus dominicus

L 8.6–10.6" | **WS** 14.1"

As the name implies, the Least Grebe is the smallest of the grebes that occur in the state. Texas is at the northern tip of this aquatic bird's range which extends southward to northern Argentina. They have long been thought of as a specialty of South Texas, but in the past twenty years, their range has expanded northward to the Austin area and the Upper Texas Coast. They are generally uncommon and prefer marshes with abundant emergent vegetation. There they can build large nests out of the marshland's decaying foliage.

Least Grebes can be identified by their very small size, slaty-gray plumage, and bright yellow eyes.

Pied-billed Grebe

Podilymbus podiceps

L 13.5" | **WS** 17-25"

Although notably larger than a Least Grebe, the Pied-billed Grebe is still a small bird. They are common winter residents statewide and uncommon and local during summer. In breeding plumage there is an obvious black band across the middle of the otherwise pale bill which gives rise to the common name. They have a rather chunky look to them with a large head and virtually no tail. Migrants and winter residents are found between September and April.

In breeding plumage they are largely brown and gray in coloration with contrasting black crown and throat. The bill is almost white with an obvious black band.

Winter birds have paler body plumage that is brown and tan with a plain silvery to yellowish bill.

Eared Grebe

Podiceps nigricollis

L 11.8–13.7" | **WS** 20.4–21.6"

Eared Grebes are common to locally abundant winter residents. In their gray and white winter plumage, they often look like puff balls sitting on the water. These birds can sometimes be found in very large concentrations with hundreds, if not thousands, on a single small lake. Eared Grebes are uncommon and local breeding birds near El Paso and in the northern Panhandle. Migrants and winter residents are found between October and April.

Winter plumaged Eared Grebes often sit high in the water with their flanks and rear end fluffed up. They have a gray crown that extends down into the white throat.

Many Eared Grebes molt into breeding plumage before migrating north. These birds can be easily identified by their black head and neck and golden ear tufts.

Clark's Grebe

Aechmophorus clarkii

L 21.6–29.5″ | **WS** 31.8–32.2″

The Clark's Grebe has increased in abundance in Texas over the past twenty years. They were once greatly outnumbered by their close cousin, the Western Grebe (*Aechmophorus occidentalis*), but now are by far the most common on the various reservoirs in the Trans-Pecos. The first nesting record for Clark's Grebe was actually a hybrid pairing with a Western Grebe in 1991, but by 2005 these birds were a regular nesting species, sometimes in large numbers at places like Balmorhea Lake and McNary Reservoir. Clark's Grebes are common to locally abundant permanent residents in the western half of the Trans-Pecos. They are amazingly vocal and have an elaborate courtship display that includes running on the surface of the water.

The bright yellow bill and white on the face that includes the red eye separate this "swan-necked" Grebe from the similar Western Grebe.

Western Grebes differ in the greenish colored bill and more extensive black on the face and upperparts.

Magnificent Frigatebird

Fregata magnificens

L 35–44.8" | **WS** 85.4–88.1"

Magnificent Frigatebirds primarily occur as post-breeding wanderers. The very long, narrow wings and very long forked tail make them easy to recognize. They are generally uncommon visitors to the coast in the summer and fall, but can be locally common. These birds are aerial specialists that spend the vast majority of the day on the wing. They pick food off the water's surface as well as steal from other birds by harassing them until they drop their prey. Magnificent Frigatebirds nest in the Caribbean and once the young fledge from the nest, they disperse away from nesting colonies. They are most often found from May to September. Despite their large size, their hollow bones make frigatebirds some of the lightest of the large seabirds in the world.

Immature birds have a solid white head, neck and breast and females are similar but with a black head. Female and immature Magnificent Frigatebirds greatly outnumber males.

Double-crested Cormorant

Phalacrocorax auritus

L 31.5″ | **WS** 46.5″

Cormorants are large water birds that feed primarily on fish. Because of this characteristic they are sometimes considered pests, certainly so at fish hatcheries and on some reservoirs that are frequented by sport fishermen. Cormorants do not have as much oil in their feathers as other waterbirds do and they can frequently be seen sitting in the sun to dry their feathers. Double-crested Cormorants are common to abundant winter residents along the coast and uncommon on inland reservoirs except in the Panhandle where they are rare. Despite the fact that they can be seen in many areas of the state in summer, these cormorants only nest in small numbers on a few reservoirs. Migrants and winter residents are in Texas from October to March.

The plumage of adults is entirely black. They can be identified by the orange bill and throat patch that has a rounded border and includes the entire chin.

Immature birds are much browner than adults with feathering on the throat and breast. The bare skin on the throat often is yellowish-orange.

Anhinga

Anhinga anhinga

L 29.5–37.4″ | **WS** 42.9″

The Anhinga is somewhat reminiscent of a slender cormorant, but has a straight dagger-like bill and longer tail. They are also fish eaters, using their bills to spear fish. Like cormorants, they lack oils in their feathers and must sit in the sun to allow them to dry. Anhingas are uncommon to locally common summer residents through the eastern third of the state southward through South Texas. Almost all of them leave the state in the winter, but a few can be found along the coast. Anhingas can be seen soaring at great heights and they have a unique shape that makes them easy to identify. These birds basically resemble a cross with their long neck, wings and tail. Migrants and summer residents are found from March to October.

The males are entirely black with white feathering on the wings. At the height of breeding plumage the bare skin of the face turns lime green and light blue. The females are similar with a tan neck and breast.

The white feathering on the wings of an Anhinga is most conspicuous when they are sitting in the sun to dry their feathers.

American White Pelican

Pelecanus erythrorhynchos

L 49.2–64.9″ | **WS** 88.1–114″

Pelicans are massive birds that are of course best known for their large bills with a flexible pouch that is used to capture fish. The American White Pelican is an uncommon to common migrant through the eastern half of the state and decidedly less common westward. They winter in large numbers along the coast and on reservoirs in the southern half of the state. Although it is not difficult to find American White Pelicans along the coast in the summer, there is only one nesting location in Texas and it is near Corpus Christi. Migrants and winter residents can be found between late September and May. White Pelicans are often confused with other large black and white birds in flight, such as Wood Storks (*Mycteria americana*) and even Whooping Cranes.

The massive orange bill combined with the entirely white body plumage makes this pelican easy to identify. The flight feathers are black, but they are often not visible except in flight.

Brown Pelican

Pelecanus occidentalis

L 39–54" | **WS** 79"

The Brown Pelican is an example of one of the great conservation success stories in Texas. They were virtually wiped out in Texas by the early 1970s because of the use of the pesticide DDT. However, they are now abundant permanent residents along the coast. This increase in abundance has brought an increase in the number of these birds found on inland reservoirs in the late summer and fall. Brown Pelicans tend to start wandering once their nesting activities are completed. These birds capture fish by diving at schools from high above the water's surface.

Juvenile and immature birds are generally dark brown overall with whitish underparts.

Brown Pelicans have the characteristic pouched bill. Breeding plumaged adults have a yellow and white head with a brown neck bisected by a white vertical stripe. In non-breeding plumage the neck is entirely white.

Great Blue Heron

Ardea herodias

L 38–54″ | **WS** 66–79″

The Great Blue Heron is the most widespread heron found in Texas. Their very large size and use of wetlands of almost any size make them a well-known bird. They are common summer residents throughout the state, although decidedly more common along the coast. The overall population at inland sites decreases in the winter as many birds migrate to coastal locations. As with most herons, Great Blue Herons develop plumes of feathers in breeding plumage and for a short period the skin on their face turns bright blue.

This breeding-plumaged bird exhibits long plumes on its head and neck as well as a bright yellow-orange bill.

In winter, these birds are gray overall and the upper mandible is dusky.

Great Egret

Ardea alba

L 40″ | **WS** 54″

The Great Egret can be found throughout the state, although it is much more common in the eastern half and along the coastal prairies. They use virtually all types of wetlands from small ponds to coastal estuaries. When northern migrants augment the resident population in the fall, large concentrations can be seen, sometimes numbering nearly 1,000 birds. Like many other herons and egrets, Great Egrets nest in colonies called rookeries. These are often found on islands in mixed colonies with other wading birds as well as cormorants and Anhingas.

In high breeding plumage, the Great Egret is a spectacular sight with the long plumes on its back and bright lime green facial skin.

Even in non-breeding plumage they are elegant birds with their clean white plumage and long black legs.

Snowy Egret

Egretta thula

L 24″ | **WS** 39″

Snowy Egrets are uncommon to common summer residents in the eastern half of the state and abundant along the coastal prairies. In the west they are uncommon migrants. These birds, along with other egrets, were heavily hunted in the late nineteenth century for their plumes that were used to decorate women's hats. This greatly reduced their overall numbers, but conservation actions have allowed the species to bounce back. These small egrets are quite attractive at all seasons with their sleek white appearance. During winter most of the Texas population is found along the coast, but they are found with increasing frequency at inland locations.

Snowy Egrets are entirely white with yellow lores and a black bill.

A characteristic feature of these birds is their black legs and bright yellow feet.

Little Blue Heron

Egretta caerulea

L 24″ | **WS** 40″

The Little Blue Heron is a common summer resident in the eastern third of the state becoming abundant along the coastal prairies. In winter they are found primarily only along the coast. These small slate-blue herons are known for their very deliberate feeding style, normally waiting for prey to come close enough to capture. Migrants and summer residents are found from March to early September.

The slaty blue plumage of the adult, including the belly, is unique among Texas waders. Look for the black-tipped gray bill and yellow-green legs.

Juvenile birds are entirely white with grayish lores and greenish-yellow legs, but as they molt into adult plumage they are splotched with dark patches.

Tricolored Heron

Egretta tricolor

L 23–27.7" | **WS** 37"

The Tricolored Heron gets its name from the white, slaty blue and rufous coloration of its plumage. They are superficially similar to the Little Blue Heron, but are more slender in shape and have a white belly. Tricolored Herons are common along the coastal prairies and can be locally abundant along the immediate coast. After breeding, these birds are known to wander inland, particularly in the eastern third of the state, but there are records from virtually all regions.

The adult is slaty-blue overall with a prominent white stripe down the front of the neck to the white breast and belly.

Contrasting strongly with the adults, immature birds are bright rufous on their necks and wings.

Reddish Egret

Egretta rufescens

L 27–31″ | **WS** 45″

The Reddish Egret is truly a coastal denizen. They nest in colonies on islands in bays and for the most part are found in saltwater habitats. They are uncommon to common although most common on the central and lower coast. The population in Texas appears to be declining and is of conservation concern. These birds are very active feeders, often running through shallow water to startle prey. However, they also will stand perfectly still with their wings spread to attract fish into the shadow produced. The Reddish Egret occurs in dark and white morphs—birds that are white as nestlings remain white and dark nestlings remain dark throughout their lives.

Adult Reddish Egrets have shaggy necks with striking bicolored bills. Dark morph birds have a gray body with rusty head and neck.

White morphs birds are entirely white with a bicolored bill. Immature birds have a black bill.

Cattle Egret

Bubulcus ibis

L 18–22″ | **WS** 35–39″

Cattle Egrets are a relatively new bird to Texas. These small egrets are native to Europe, Africa, and Asia and have colonized many other areas, including North America. The first Cattle Egrets were found in Texas in 1954. They are now abundant along the coastal prairies and locally common inland, although rather locally in the western half of the state. Unlike most other herons, Cattle Egrets are equally at home in upland areas away from water and as their name implies they are frequently seen in the company of livestock.

Breeding plumaged adults have orange plumes on head, breast, and back and the bill and legs are yellow.

Non-breeding plumage is entirely white with a yellow bill and black legs.

Green Heron

Butorides virescens

L 17″ | **WS** 26″

Unlike most of the other herons found in Texas, the Green Heron is a solitary and much more inconspicuous bird. They do not nest in colonies and are most often encountered in dense vegetation on the edges of wetlands. Their dark plumage helps keep them camouflaged as they sit quietly waiting to ambush prey. They have a more compact body than most herons, giving them a chunky appearance. They are common permanent residents in the eastern half of the state becoming uncommon and local further west.

The adult Green Heron is a striking with its dark chestnut neck and dark green upperparts.

Yellow-crowned Night-Heron

Nyctanassa violacea

L 24″ | **WS** 42″

The adult Yellow-crowned Night-Heron is unmistakable with this black head contrasting strongly with the gray plumage of the neck and body. As the name implies, these birds are most active at night. However, they also forage during the day. They are crustacean specialists and prey on small crabs and crayfish in particular. Yellow-crowned Night Herons are common permanent residents along the coastal prairies and uncommon inland through the eastern half of the state during the spring and summer. In flight, the feet and lower part of the legs extend beyond the tail.

Adults have a yellow crown that extends into two long plumes. The yellow-white cheek patch contrasts against the otherwise black face.

Immature birds are brownish-gray and heavily marked with lighter coloration on the underparts giving it a streaked appearance.

White Ibis

Eudocimus albus

L 22–26.7″ | **WS** 38.9″

The White Ibis is a common sight along the coastal prairies where they are often encountered in large flocks. These birds often forage in groups probing into the mud with their long, downcurved bills. They will also feed in upland habitats searching for grasshoppers and other insects.

Adults are white with the exception of black tips to the outer primaries that are only visible in flight. Their facial skin and legs are pinkish-red.

Immature birds are largely brown with white underparts.

White-faced Ibis

Plegadis chihi

L 18.1–22″ | **WS** 37″

The White-faced Ibis is by far the most common dark ibis found in Texas. They are fairly common permanent residents on the coastal prairies with the population increasing in the winter when migrants from the Great Plains arrive. The White-faced Ibis is an uncommon to common migrant through the state, although generally found west of the pine forest of East Texas. Migrants are often encountered in flocks up to 100 individuals. They favor areas of shallow water and often feed in groups. In adults, a feature that distinguishes this bird from the very similar Glossy Ibis (*Plegadis falcinellus*) is its red eye.

Breeding plumaged adults may look black from a distance, but the plumage is actually dark chestnut with iridescent green. The bill is grayish and down curved. The facial skin can vary from dark to pink and can be bordered by white feathers.

Non-breeding adults and immature birds are dark olive-brown with white mottling on head and neck.

Roseate Spoonbill

Platalea ajaja

L 27.9–33.8" | **WS** 47.2–51.1"

One of the most striking birds found on the Texas coast is the Roseate Spoonbill. As the name implies, they have a long bill that is spatulate on the end resembling a spoon. They have baleen-like filaments in their bill and feed in shallow water straining out small invertebrates and other prey items. These birds have a strong tendency to wander after the nesting period and that includes inland where there are records from all regions of the state. These wanderers include both adults and immature birds. The unfeathered head of the adult add to the unmistakable look of this species.

The spoon-shaped bill of this bird make it hard to mistake. In breeding plumage they have pink body plumage with even brighter pink wings and an orange tail. Immature birds are much paler in overall color and the head is covered with white feathers.

Black Vulture

Coragyps atratus

L 25″ | **WS** 59″

Vultures are readily identified by their dark body plumage and unfeathered heads. They have short legs and relatively weak feet that do not allow them to grasp and carry away food items. As a result, they are very well known for standing on the side of the road feeding on roadkill. Black Vultures are common to abundant permanent residents in the eastern half of the state including the eastern Hill Country and all of the South Texas Brush Country. They range west into the Trans-Pecos only along the Rio Grande although they are can be found as far west as Presidio.

The black plumage with an unfeathered black head identifies this species. In flight the pale outer primaries are easily visible.

Turkey Vulture

Cathartes aura

L 25–32″ | **WS** 68.5″

Although the Turkey Vulture is familiar to anyone living in Texas, they actually have an interesting pattern of occurrence in the state. They are common to abundant summer residents in all areas, but they leave most of the western half of the state in winter. Oddly, at the same latitudes farther east, they become more common as migrating birds from farther north arrive for the winter. Turkey Vultures are particularly common in open areas where their acute vision and sense of smell help them locate carrion. They, along with the Black Vulture, provide a great service by cleaning up dead animals.

The red, unfeathered head of an adult Turkey Vulture is reminiscent of a Wild Turkey and, thus, the common name.

In flight these birds hold their wings in a slight V formation with the darker body contrasting slightly with the paler flight feathers.

Osprey

Pandion haliaetus

L 22" | **WS** 59–71"

The Osprey is probably best known for the ability to capture fish. They have very long claws that are strongly curved that allow them to grab and then carry these favored prey items to a perch. They are uncommon to rare migrants through the state and only common as winter residents along the coast and at large reservoirs in the eastern half. Osprey is a surprisingly rare nesting species in Texas despite its abundance along most of the remainder of the Gulf Coast. Over the past ten years Ospreys have begun to winter, in small numbers, farther north and west than they did historically. They are now a more regular sight as far west as the central Trans-Pecos.

Ospreys have very long wings and are brown above and white below. The white head is marked with a wide brown eye stripe.

White-tailed Kite

Elanus leucurus

L 12.5–14.9″ | **WS** 42.1″

The White-tailed Kite is an uncommon denizen of the grassland and the coastal prairies north through the oaks and prairies of east-central Texas. In recent years this species has been found in many areas outside of the traditional range, but in relatively small numbers. The birds that have been found on the Rolling Plains and the west Trans-Pecos could be the first sign of a range expansion into these areas. These elegant birds are known for their habit of hovering in place waiting for the right moment to drop on prey.

The long narrow wings and tail give these birds agility while on the wing. They are gray above and white below with obvious black patches on the shoulders.

Mississippi Kite

Ictinia mississippiensis

L 13.3–14.5″ | **WS** 35″

Mississippi Kites seem most at home on the wing and are both graceful and agile while capturing large flying insects. They are uncommon to locally common summer residents across the northern half of the state becoming more uncommon and local south through the eastern half. Mississippi Kites are found in open woodland and are commonly seen in towns where large trees are available for nest sites. These birds can be highly territorial and defensive around the nest including toward humans. Migrants and summer residents can be found between April and October.

Adults are gray overall with a paler head and long wings that extend beyond the tail when perched.

In flight, the slender wings and a long tail are evident. The secondaries of the wing are obviously paler and provide a good field mark.

Bald Eagle

Haliaeetus leucocephalus

L 28–38″ | **WS** 80″

Another of the success stories of conservation efforts in North America is the Bald Eagle. These birds were strongly impacted by DDT contamination, which caused their eggs to be fragile and easily broken by the incubating adults. In the 1970s, Bald Eagles were all but gone as a nesting bird in Texas, but they have recovered and there are now more than 300 active nest sites. These breeding birds are found primarily in the eastern half of the state, although new nesting sites in the west have been discovered in recent years. They are much more common and widespread in the winter when they can be found almost statewide, including in the grassland of the Trans-Pecos. Although they are often thought of as fish-eaters, they will also feed on mammals and even carrion.

Immatures are largely brown with varying amounts of white in the underparts.

The adult is an iconic symbol in the United States, with its white head and tail contrasting with the brown body.

Northern Harrier

Circus hudsonius

L 19″ | **WS** 43″

Northern Harriers seem to effortlessly glide over open grassland as they search for prey. These long-winged and long-tailed hawks are uncommon to locally common migrants and winter residents in all areas of the state. Although Northern Harriers are usually solitary hunters like most raptors, it is not unusual to see several birds hunting in the same area. In Texas, immature birds far outnumber adults and because of the similarity of plumage between immature birds and adult females it appears that males are far outnumbered. Migrants begin to arrive in September and most leave by late April. A few will remain into the summer, but nesting is rare.

Adult males are easily recognized by the silvery gray of the head and upperparts. They have a conspicuous white rump, black primaries and white underparts.

Adult females are largely brown in color, but the underparts are fairly heavily streaked, unlike immature birds that have tan underparts with very few markings.

Sharp-shinned Hawk

Accipiter striatus

L 11.5" | **WS** 19"

Sharp-shinned Hawks are in a group of raptors known as Accipiters. These birds are found in woodland and forest habitats and prey specifically on other birds. Rounded wings and long tails help them maneuver between trees as they frequently capture their prey on the wing. Sharp-shinned Hawks are also known for capturing birds that have been attracted to feeders. There are two common Accipiters in Texas, the Cooper's Hawk and the Sharp-shinned Hawk. The Sharp-shinned is smaller with a noticeably square-shaped tail. Females tend to be larger than males and there is some overlap between the size of a small male Cooper's Hawk and a large female Sharp-shinned. They are uncommon winter residents occurring mainly between September and March. These small hawks are very rare in summer in the pine forests of East Texas and in the upper elevations of the mountains in the Trans-Pecos.

Immature birds (right) are largely brown above and heavily mottled with white. Below they are white and with brown streaking. They have smallish rounded heads and square tails. Adults are slate-gray above and the white underparts are heavily barred with red.

Cooper's Hawk

Accipiter cooperii

L 15″ | **WS** 30″

The Cooper's Hawk is the Accipiter that is more likely to be encountered in Texas during the breeding season. Although they are generally uncommon and somewhat local, they nest in most areas in the southern half of the state and northward to the Red River and in the forested eastern third. They are generally found in all areas during the winter. Cooper's Hawks are larger than Sharp-shinned Hawks and have a rounded tail. They are found primarily in woodlands and feed largely on birds. Migrants arrive in September and most move northward by early March.

Adults have the same basic plumage pattern as the Sharp-shinned Hawk, but with a larger, somewhat square head and a rounded tail.

Immature birds are brown above with some white mottling and white below heavily streaked with brown.

Red-shouldered Hawk

Buteo lineatus

L 20″ | **WS** 40″

The Red-shouldered Hawk is a forest hawk that is found primarily in the eastern half of the state, but can be found along wooded rivers throughout the Hill Country. They tend to wander in the fall and are sometimes found far from their normal range. It is a medium-sized hawk with a compact build with rounded wings and a medium length tail. They are very vocal and are often detected by their calls. The plumage of an adult Red-shouldered Hawks is dominated by dark reds and browns that are ideally adapted for life in the low light conditions of the forest allowing them to be inconspicuous when perched.

Adults have a black and white checkered upperparts and white below heavily marked with rusty bands. As the name implies, they also have an obvious red shoulder patch.

Immature birds resemble a number of other hawks, but tend to be heavily marked below and have prominent pale crescents on the tips of their wings and long tails.

Broad-winged Hawk

Buteo platypterus

L 15″ | **WS** 34″

Broad-winged Hawks are probably best known for the spectacular migrations along the coast, particularly in fall. These small hawks winter in South America, but they do not fly across the Gulf of Mexico. Each spring and fall flocks that can include thousands of birds stream overhead as they make their way along the coastline. These flocks are often larger in the fall when the birds raised that year join the adults. They are uncommon migrants through the eastern half of the state and rare in the west. Broad-winged Hawks are also common nesting birds in the east, where they are found in woodland habitats. Spring migrants can be found from mid-March to mid-May and from late August to mid-October in the fall.

They are brown above with a rufous chest that gives way to a white belly barred with rufous. There is a black border to all of the flight feathers that contrasts with the white underwing.

Immature birds are brown above and white below. The neck and breast are very heavily marked with brown.

Swainson's Hawk

Buteo swainsoni

L 19–22" | **WS** 47.2–54.3"

Swainson's Hawks are found in the open grassland of the western United States. These hawks also winter in South America, but since they are coming from the West they do not necessarily make it as far east as the Gulf. In the spring, it is not uncommon to see a flock of these birds following a tractor on the High Plains picking up grasshoppers or rodents disturbed by the farmer's actions. They are uncommon summer residents in the western two-thirds of the state. Spring migrants can be found from mid-March to mid-May and from late August to early November in the fall.

Adults have brown upperparts and white underparts that contrast strongly with a rufous chest. There is a small percentage where the body plumage is entirely dark brown.

Immature birds are largely white below but they are heavily streaked with brown on the sides of the neck down through the chest. The underwings, and sometimes the belly, can have a wash of tan.

White-tailed Hawk

Geranoaetus albicaudatus

L 18.1–22.8" | **WS** 51.9"

White-tailed Hawks have a vast range through the tropics and reach the northern edge of their distribution in Texas. These very attractive hawks are found in the open habitats along the coastal prairies as far north as Galveston Bay. Being birds of these grassland, they know that fires are an opportunity for easy hunting. White-taileds are attracted to the columns of smoke and swoop down to capture rodents and reptiles fleeing the leading edge of fires.

Adults are spectacular with pearly gray upperparts and bright white below. Not surprisingly, they have a white tail with a prominent black bar near the tip.

Immature birds are very different and mostly very dark brown. They have an obvious white patch on the breast and a heavily barred tail.

Zone-tailed Hawk

Buteo albonotatus

L 17.7–22" | **WS** 46.8–55.1"

Mimicry does not often come to mind when describing a hawk, but it is apt for the Zone-tailed Hawk. These hawks are solid black and soar on long wings with a long tail and can be easily mistaken for a Turkey Vulture. On closer inspection they are easily identified as a hawk with a feathered head, yellow on the base of the bill and a tail barred with white. The Turkey Vulture is far more numerous than this hawk and the similarity in appearance allow these birds to closely approach inattentive prey. They are uncommon summer residents in the southwestern part of the state and eastward across the Hill Country. They can be found from late March to mid-October.

Long, narrow wings are reminiscent of a Turkey Vulture, but the large round head and yellow base to the bill are features of a hawk.

Red-tailed Hawk

Buteo jamaicensis

L 20″ | **WS** 48.5″

By far the most widespread and familiar raptor that occurs in Texas is the Red-tailed Hawk. They can be seen in all areas of the state and their habit of sitting on power poles and other open perches makes them easy to observe. Adult Red-tailed Hawks are pale below and generally have some brown markings on the belly, but the birds found in the southwestern part of the state lack this characteristic. There are dark morph birds found in the western United States and these birds can be seen in Texas in the winter. As a result, there is astounding variety in the appearance of this species. Red-tailed Hawks are common year-round residents in the state, but they become locally abundant in the winter when birds from farther north join the resident populations. Wintering population can increase considerably when local rodent populations are high.

The most striking feature is the bright red tail of an adult.

Immature birds are white below with a band of dark streaks across the belly. This features varied greatly and some birds can have extensive streaking below.

Most of the dark morph Red-tailed Hawks found in Texas are from the breeding populations in the western United States and Canada.

Clapper Rail

Rallus longirostris

L 12.5–16″ | **WS** 20″

The salt marshes along the coast are home to the Clapper Rail. Although rails, as a general rule, remain hiddenmost of the time, these medium-size birds can often be seen foraging along the edges of dense vegetation or out in shallow water. Even so, Clapper Rails are heard much more often than they are seen. Their calls include a loud series of up to ten *kek* notes that often get louder as though the bird is becoming agitated. The very similar looking King Rail (*Rallus elegans*) is also found on the coast, but they are found in freshwater wetlands. These two species are closely related and often difficult to identify.

The stocky build, thick neck, and long bill identify this as a rail. The large size with a buffy breast and black-and-white barred belly of this bird indicate Clapper Rail.

Virginia Rail

Rallus limicola

L 9″ | **WS** 14″

The Virginia Rail is one of two rails that are commonly found in Texas away from the coast. Even though these birds look similar in structure and coloration to a Clapper Rail, they are much smaller. They are most often detected by their calls that are best described as a series of grunts, but when excited they also give a series of *kik* notes. These birds are fairly common breeders in the Panhandle and occur as migrants and winter residents elsewhere in the state. Migrants from further north begin to arrive in September and most return north during March.

The long reddish bill and sticky posture help identify this species. They have a prominent gray cheek that contrasts with the brown crown and neck. Adults are mainly brown above with a rufous breast and barred belly.

Sora

Porzana carolina

L 8.5″ | **WS** 14″

Like the Virginia Rail, the Sora can be found throughout the state. These small, gray rails belong to a group of small rails with short bills called crakes. They are probably the most common rail to be found in Texas in the winter. As with other rails the call is often how these birds are detected. Soras give a number of high-pitched calls including a descending whinny and loud *keek* notes.

These birds are small and stocky with a short yellow bill. They are mainly brown above and gray below.

Common Gallinule

Gallinula galeata

L 13″ | **WS** 23″

The Common Gallinule is similar to the much more common and widespread American Coot. Unlike the coot, these birds are found only in fresh water and typically in wetlands with abundant emergent vegetation. They are much more likely to be seen in shallow water or along the shoreline than out on a lake or in deep water. They are common to locally abundant along the coastal prairies and in the Lower Rio Grande Valley year-round and much more uncommon and local inland, particularly in the western half of the state. Until recently they were considered as the same species as the Common Moorhen (*Gallinula choropus*) of Eurasia and was listed under that common name.

The white feather tips along the flanks forms a line over the folded wing on the otherwise black body. They have a red bill that is tipped in yellow.

Purple Gallinule

Porphyrio martinicus

L 10.6–14.1″ | **WS** 21.6″

The bright plumage of the Purple Gallinule makes it a favorite among birders visiting the Texas coast. They are uncommon to locally common summer residents in freshwater marshes throughout the coastal prairies and in the Lower Rio Grande Valley. The preferred habitat is ponds and other wetlands with floating vegetation. The very long toes of the Purple Gallinule allow their weight to be distributed in such a way so that these birds can walk on lily pads. They are much more agile than other rails that occur in Texas and it is not uncommon to see them climbing up in shrubs in search for food. Migrants and summer residents are found between April and September.

The bright blue and purple plumage of an adult makes this bird easy to identify. They also have long yellow legs, greenish wings, and white under the tail.

American Coot

Fulica americana

L 16″ | **WS** 24–28″

During the winter, American Coots are among the most ubiquitous waterbirds found in Texas. They can be found in wetlands throughout the state as well as in the bays along the coast. On occasion, they can be found in rafts of thousands on the large reservoirs in the eastern half of the state. A large percentage of the population migrates out of the state each spring, but American Coots are still easy to find. Coots are herbivores and they will frequently leave the water to graze on the surrounding vegetation, including turf grass.

The bright white bill of the American Coot contrasts strongly with the black head and gray body. A white shield covers the forehead which has a maroon patch on the top.

Sandhill Crane

Antigone canadensis

L 47″ | **WS** 78.5″

The trumpeting call of the Sandhill Crane can be heard for up to a mile away. These birds are common migrants and locally abundant winter residents in Texas. More than 10,000 roost in the shallow lakes at Muleshoe National Wildlife Refuge each winter and the cacophony these birds make when they leave for feeding areas each morning is not to be missed. The wintering population is divided between the playa (shallow wetlands) and grassland of northwest Texas and the coastal prairies. Even though these are the primary wintering areas in the state, Sandhill Cranes can show up almost anywhere else. Migrants and winter residents can be seen between early October and mid-March.

The tall stature and uniform gray plumage make an adult easy to identify. Although herons are occasionally referred to as cranes, the unfeathered red crown eliminates all herons.

These cranes fly with their necks fully extended and often in large groups.

Whooping Crane

Grus americana

L 59″ | **WS** 90.1″

Whooping Cranes are an iconic symbol of conservation in the United States. There were only 14 individuals left in the late 1930s and now there are almost 250 birds in the natural population. Even so, they are not safe from threats to the continued existence of the species. Conservation efforts have included attempts to establish a second flock that winters outside of Texas. One of the biggest concerns for the continued health of the natural flock is the increase in salinity in the marshes where they winter. This has a direct impact on the quality of the habitat and their food. The natural population nests in northern Alberta, Canada and winters on the Texas Coast in the vicinity of Aransas National Wildlife Refuge. Migrants and winter residents can be found between late October and mid-April.

They are the tallest bird in North America. Adults are mostly white with black wingtips that are often hidden. They have an unfeathered red crown and face.

Immature birds have tan feathering on the head and neck that extends irregularly into the white body plumage. They also lack the distinctive red skin on the head.

American Oystercatcher

Haematopus palliatus

L 15.7–17.3" | **WS** 35"

One of the most fascinating birds found on the Texas coast is the American Oystercatcher. They are quite large for a shorebird and their feeding strategy of flipping over possible hiding places for small crabs and other prey items is noteworthy. They also use their bright red, thin bill to open mollusks, which, of course, gives rise to the common name. American Oystercatchers are locally common along the beaches, man-made islands, and tidal flats of the coast south to Corpus Christi and are much more uncommon and localized farther south. With numbers declining, Texas harbors one of the most significant remaining populations.

Unmistakable with their long bright red bill and eye ring contrasting against the black head. Their upperparts are brown and they have rather short, stout legs.

Black-necked Stilt

Himantopus mexicanus

L 13.7–15.3″ | **WS** 27.9″

The starkly black-and-white plumage of the Black-necked Stilt along with the very long pink legs makes this bird easy to identify. Despite these features, they have a relatively short bill which requires them to tip down in order to pick up food items. They are common along the coastal prairies year-round, though fewer in winter. In the summer the nesting population is found in the northwestern quarter of the state as well as the El Paso area where they are uncommon and local. In the Panhandle and South Plains, they are found around rain-filled ponds (called playas) and as a result, the availability of nesting areas varied greatly from year to year. Away from the coast Black-necked Stilts can be found from April through September.

The slender body and very long legs gives them a long appearance. The males are jet black backs whereas the females have a wash of brown.

American Avocet

Recurvirostra americana

L 16.9–18.5″ | **WS** 32.2″

The American Avocet is one of the most beautiful of North America's shorebirds, particularly in breeding plumage. They are related to the Black-necked Stilt and share the long legs but are easily separated by their white body plumage. American Avocets also have much longer bills that are slightly upturned at the tip, most obviously in females. Avocets often feed by holding their bills very slightly open and sweeping them back and forth through the water. They are common to locally abundant winter residents along the coast, particularly south of Matagorda Bay. During the summer they are locally common on the High Plains when playas have water and thus provide habitat. Migrants and summer residents are found between mid-March and early November.

In breeding plumage, the head, neck and upper breast have a buffy-orange coloration. The body is otherwise white except for the black and white wings.

In the winter, the head and neck are pale gray, often looking white and not contrasting with the body. The straight bill identifies this bird as a male. Females have a more curved bill.

Black-bellied Plover

Pluvialis squatarola

L 11″ | **WS** 23″

Black-bellied Plovers are a common sight on coastal beaches during the winter. Although in a group of shorebirds that are mostly small, this plover is the largest. In general, the plover group is characterized by having round heads and short bills and are very active, usually running and then stopping abruptly. Black-bellied Plovers have dramatically different summer and winter plumages, both of which can be seen in Texas. They are uncommon to common winter residents along the coastal prairies and uncommon to rare farther inland. A few can be found at any season, but they do not nest in Texas. Migrants and winter residents are found between September and May.

Winter plumage is overall gray-brown with a thick black bill and black legs. Upperparts are mottled brown and the underparts are distinctly whiter.

In the spring, summer plumaged birds can be seen in their striking black and white plumage.

Wilson's Plover

Charadrius wilsonia

L 6.2–7.8″ | **WS** 16.1″

Wilson's Plover is a specialist on beaches and mudflats along the immediate coast. A single wide breast band and rather thick bill are keys to identification. While they can be seen running along the surfs edge, they are more common foraging in the seaweed and other debris above the tide line. They are uncommon to locally common summer residents along the entire coast becoming rare and more localized in the winter. The nesting population arrives in March and has mostly departed by the end of September.

The male is brown above with a black breast band. They also have a black border across the front of the brown crown and between the eye and the base of the bill extending into the cheek.

Females are similar to males, but they are lighter brown in color and lack the black highlights.

Semipalmated Plover

Charadrius semipalmatus

L 7″ | **WS** 14″

The Semipalmated Plover is perhaps the most common of the small, banded plovers to be found in Texas. The name refers to the partial webbing between the toes. They are uncommon to locally abundant in winter along the coastal prairies and can be found on beaches, mud flats, flooded fields and other very shallow wetlands. They are uncommon migrants through the entire state although less common in the far west. A few of these birds may linger through the summer, but they do not nest. Migrants begin to arrive in early July and the last of them will depart for the breeding grounds in early May.

Breeding plumaged adults are crisply plumaged with brown upperparts and white below. They have a prominent white eyebrow and neck ring with black on the face and breast band of males. In this plumage, the base of the bill and legs can be bright orange.

During most of their stay in Texas they are dull brown above with a black or brown breast band. The bill has a dull orange base and the legs are yellowish.

Piping Plover

Charadrius melodus

L 6.6–7″ | **WS** 15.3″

The Piping Plover is listed as Endangered by the U.S. Fish and Wildlife Service. The birds that spend the winter in Texas breed on the Great Plains. They are most often encountered along the beaches and bayside tidal flats along the coast. They are reminiscent of a very pale Semipalmated Plover, but they often lack the complete breast band. Migrants and winter residents are found between August and May.

In the spring they molt into breeding plumage with a black strip on the front of the crown, black partial to complete breast band and an orange base to the bill.

During most of their stay in Texas they are very pale above including the partial breast band. The bill is very short and black and the legs are yellow.

Killdeer

Charadrius vociferus

L 9" | **WS** 18.5"

Killdeer are not dependent on water to successfully raise their young. These plovers are found in upland habitats and around the edges of freshwater wetlands. They are particularly adaptable and seem to coexist in close proximity to people. The common name is an approximation of the calls that include a rolling *kill-dee* and a *dee-dee-dee*. When their nest or young are threatened, they spread their colorful tails and flounder on the ground. Known as a "broken wing act," this behavior is meant to to distract potential predators. This is a common distraction technique for birds and flashing the red-orange rump seems to be very effective.

Adult Killdeer have two prominent black breast bands across their otherwise white underparts. The upperparts are brown and they have a strongly marked head.

Spotted Sandpiper

Actitis macularia

L 7.5″ | **WS** 15″

Spotted Sandpipers almost constantly bob the back half of the body while foraging. This distinctive behavior is a good first clue when trying to identify these birds as is the fluttery, stiff flight style. When in breeding plumage, their white underparts are heavily spotted with brown; however, Spotted Sandpipers are in winter plumage for the largest part of their time in Texas. They are common migrants throughout the state and uncommon to common winter residents in the southern two-thirds. Migrants and winter residents can be found from early July through late May. Small numbers will linger into the summer as well.

Breeding plumage similar to winter except white underparts heavily spotted with brown and the bill and legs become bright orange.

While in winter plumage they are brown above and white below with a brown wash on the sides of the upper breast.

Greater Yellowlegs

Tringa melanoleuca

L 11–13.5″ | **WS** 23″

There are two species of yellowlegs and both commonly occur in Texas. Both are very similar in coloration and structural differences are the key in identification. The Greater Yellowlegs is of course larger with a long, slightly upturned bill. They tend to be darker overall with more barring on the underparts. They are common migrants throughout the state and uncommon in winter through the southern two-thirds. Even though these birds nest primarily in Canada, the first fall migrants reach Texas in July and lingering spring migrants can still be present in June.

Yellowlegs are slender in stature with a long neck and yellow legs. Greater Yellowlegs have a slightly upturned bill.

In winter plumage they are whiter below with varying amounts of dark markings.

Willet

Tringa semipalmata

L 12.9–16″ | **WS** 27.5″

There are two distinct populations of Willet in Texas—the birds that spend the winter along the coast breed on the Great Plains and those that nest on the coast spend the the winter farther south. It has been suggested that these two populations should be treated as separate species. Willets are common along the coast throughout the year and in the spring and fall there are birds from the breeding and wintering populations are both present. Inland migrants can be found between mid-July and mid-September and late March to early May.

Winter plumaged birds are gray overall with a thick bill that is black with a gray base.

The bold black and white flight feathers of the Willet are distinctive and an excellent field mark.

Lesser Yellowlegs

Tringa flavipes

L 10″ | **WS** 23–27″

The Lesser Yellowlegs, as its name implies, is a smaller and more slender shorebird than its cousin the Greater Yellowlegs. The very long, bright yellow legs are easily to see under most conditions and these birds are very active when feeding, often running short distances. They can be found in every month of the year with early fall migrants arriving in July and lingering spring migrants still present in June.

They have a slender build with a long neck and a medium length bill. The bill is black and rather thin. Very similar to Greater Yellowlegs but with less barring on underparts.

Immature and winter plumaged adults are more uniform in coloration on the back and underparts.

Long-billed Curlew

Numenius americanus

L 19.6–25.5" | **WS** 10.2–12.2

The Long-billed Curlew is a very large shorebird that can be found in wetlands as well as in open grassland. They have long to very long bills with adult females sporting the longest bills and immature birds have the shortest. The grassland of the northern Panhandle is the only place in Texas where these birds nest in the state and even there they are uncommon and local. Most of the wintering birds are found along the coastal prairies, but a few can be found in agricultural areas and grassland inland. Migrants and winter residents can be found from July through mid-May.

The very long, down curved bill is a strong field mark. They have buffy plumage that is more heavily marked with dark brown and black on the upperparts.

Marbled Godwit

Limosa fedoa

L 16.5–18.8″ | **WS** 31″

The Marbled Godwit is very similar in color to the Long-billed Curlew, but their bills are very different. Godwits also have long bills, but they have a gentle upturn. Godwits feed by probing deep into sediments with their long bills. The Marbled Godwit is an uncommon migrant through the eastern two-thirds of the state and less common farther west. They are also common to uncommon winter residents on the coastal prairies. Migrants and winter residents can be found between August and early May.

They have an upturned bill that is pink with a black outer half. The body is buffy with black mottling on the upperparts. In breeding plumage the underparts are scalloped with fine black lines as well.

Ruddy Turnstone

Arenaria interpres

L 7″ | **WS** 21″

The Ruddy Turnstone is a small sandpiper with short legs that flips over rocks and other debris in search of food. When in Texas, they are primarily in winter plumage, but there is considerable variability in the amount of red in their feathering. They molt in the late winter and early spring into their spectacular breeding plumage, which is red and black on the body with a boldly patterned head. Ruddy Turnstones are common winter residents along the coast and can be found on beaches as well as jetties and seawalls. Despite this abundance, they are rarely detected as migrants away from the coast. These interesting shorebirds occur in the state between September and May.

The bright summer plumage is unmistakable with the red and black feathering on the upperparts and black and white head.

Some birds in winter plumage are primarily gray and brown above, including the head, with a black bib. Others have a varying amount of red feathers on the back.

Sanderling

Calidris alba

L 7.5″ | **WS** 13.5–16″

The Sanderling is the most abundant and obvious shorebird found on Texas's surfside beaches. They follow the surf in and out foraging for invertebrates in the sand. They are much more common in the winter, but some remain during the summer even though they do not nest in the state. Although they are by far most commonly seen on beaches, they can also be found on jetties and tidal flats. They have dramatically different breeding and nonbreeding plumages, but most of the birds that summer in Texas never molt completely into summer garb. The migrants and winter residents occur between mid-July and May. Despite the abundance of this bird on the winter grounds, migrants at inland locations are uncommon to rare.

Many molt into breeding plumage before migrating in the spring. They become rufous with black mottling on the upperparts, head and breast. The brightness of the rufous varies considerably.

Sanderlings are primarily white with pale gray on their upperparts. The bill and legs are black.

Least Sandpiper

Calidris minutilla

L 5.5″ | **WS** 10.5″

Least Sandpipers are the smallest sandpiper found in Texas, but there are a number of closely related species that are not much bigger. These sandpipers are known as "peeps." Least Sandpipers have rather short legs and when foraging they have a crouching posture that makes them inconspicuous. They are common to abundant migrants and winter residents along the coastal prairies and uncommon in winter farther inland. In the Panhandle, Least Sandpipers are rare in winter. Migrants and winter residents are found from July through mid-May with a few lingering into early June.

The yellow legs are diagnostic among the small sandpipers referred to as "peeps." Adults have upperparts that are mottled with rufous, brown, and black and they are white below with heavy streaking on the breast. The bill is slightly down curved.

Adults in winter plumage and juveniles lack rufous tones and the breast is very lightly streaked.

Long-billed Dowitcher

Limnodromus scolopaceus

L 11.4″ | **WS** 18.1″

The Long-billed Dowitcher is a common migrant that can be encountered in all areas of Texas. They use their long bill to probe deep in the mud and often forage in small groups with all of the bird rapidly teetering up and down like sewing machines as they forage. Long-billed Dowitchers are far more likely to be found in freshwater habitats, although they will tolerate brackish water as well. They are uncommon to common migrants as well as winter residents along the coastal prairies. Farther inland they become increasingly rare during winter, but will often linger in these areas well into December before continuing south. Migrants and winter residents are present from July through May with a few lingering into early June.

The most prominent feature of these birds is the long, straight bill. In winter plumage they are predominantly gray with drab yellow legs.

In breeding plumage, they are much more richly colored with rufous and brown on the upperparts and rufous wash over the breast and upper belly.

Wilson's Snipe

Gallinago delicata

L 11.5" | **WS** 17"

Wilson's Snipe rely on their intricately marked plumage to provide camouflage and avoid predators. They will often sit very still until the last minute before flying. When flushed a sharp call is given as they fly low to the ground in an irregular pattern. Wilson Snipe is a common migrant throughout the state and common winter resident in the east becoming more uncommon and local in the west. Migrants and winter residents are present from August through mid-May.

The upperparts are dark and heavily mottled with black, brown and some rufous. The head is striped and the neck and breast heavily streaked with brown. The flanks are heavily barred and the bill is long and straight.

Wilson's Phalarope

Phalaropus tricolor

L 8.6–9.4″ | **WS** 16.5″

Phalaropes are among the most interesting of our shorebirds in several ways. While they can be seen feeding as any other shorebird, probing in the mud as they walk along, they also swim briskly in a circle, spinning on the surface of deeper water creating a vortex in order to bring food items up to the surface. In an unusual switch, the female is brightly plumaged and the male is drab. The less conspicuous male incubates the eggs and cares for the young alone. There are three species of phalarope, but the Wilson's is by far the most common to occur in Texas. They are common to abundant migrants in all areas of the state and can be found in very large migrating flocks. Migrants are found during April and May and from July through October.

In breeding plumage the female has a gray and maroon back, a black eye stripe that becomes maroon on the sides of the neck, and a buffy-orange neck and breast. The male is similar but with considerably muted colors.

Winter plumaged birds are pale gray overall with a thin, needle-like bill.

Herring Gull

Larus argentatus

L 24″ | **WS** 55.5″

Of the large gulls, the Herring Gull is the most frequently encountered in Texas. It takes four years for a Herring Gull to reach adult plumage and they can be quite variable in appearance during this transition. First and second year birds are the most common found in Texas, but all age classes are represented. They are common winter residents along the coast where can be found along beaches, tidal flats, freshwater wetlands as well as landfills. They are generally rare inland, but can be locally uncommon on the large reservoirs in the eastern half of the state. Herring Gulls are uncommon to rare in summer along the coast, but there are only two nesting records. Migrants and winter residents are found between October and March.

Adults have a medium gray mantle and the remainder of the body is white. They have pink legs and a yellow bill with a red spot. The wings are tipped with black and the outer primaries have a white spot as well.

They are large, dwarfing the other normally occurring gulls found in Texas. Juvenile and first year birds are mottled brown and gray with pink legs. The upperparts have a checkered appearance. The bill can be entirely black or have a pink base.

Bonaparte's Gull

Chroicocephalus philadelphia

L 13″ | **WS** 30.5″

The Bonaparte's Gull is the smallest gull regularly found in Texas. Graceful in flight, they can be mistaken for a tern at first glance. This bird was named after Charles Bonaparte, a nephew of Napoleon, who moved to New Jersey after the French Revolution. He played an important role in American ornithology, primarily in the understanding of relationships between species. Bonaparte's Gull is an uncommon to common migrant throughout the state and a common winter resident in the eastern two-thirds, becoming rare and local farther west. Migrants and winter residents are present from late October to late March.

Breeding plumaged birds have an entirely black head, but in winter it is white with a bold spot behind the eye. The mantle is pale gray contrasting with the clean white primaries which are tipped with black.

Juveniles and much more intricately marked with a dark M shape on the upper wings and a black tip to the tail.

Laughing Gull

Leucophaeus atricilla

L 16″ | **WS** 36–47″

The Laughing Gull is the ubiquitous gull along the Texas coast and their raucous calls make it easy to see how they got their name. They are the only species of gull that normally nests in the state. Although generally thought of as a strictly coastal species, Laughing Gulls do wander inland after the breeding season. There are records from all areas of the state and they can even be uncommon on the large reservoirs in the southeastern portion. Although they are abundant throughout out the year along the coast there is evidence that part of the population migrates south to southern Mexico and Central America for the winter.

They have a dark gray mantle with black wingtips. Breeding plumaged birds have a black head with prominent white eye crescents and the bill is dark reddish.

In winter plumage the adults loose the black head, although there are varying amounts of dark on the head, and the bill is black.

Immature birds are more uniformly gray overall with a darker gray mantle.

Ring-billed Gull

Larus delawarensis

L 19″ | **WS** 43.5″

Away from the coast the Ring-billed Gull is by far the most common gull found in Texas in winter. These birds can occur in very large numbers at reservoirs and landfills. They frequently move between feeding locations and can be seen in seemingly unlikely places. These birds can be found year-round, but they do not nest any closer to Texas than South Dakota. It takes three years for these birds to reach adult plumage and as a result they can be quite variable in appearance. They are by far most commonly encountered as a migrant or winter resident and as such the best time to look for them is between August and April.

Juvenile birds are heavily mottled with brown overall, but particularly on the back. The bill is mainly black, but with a pale base.

First and second winter birds share some characteristics. The back is gray, the head and neck are spotted with gray, and the bill is pink with a black tip. Second-winter birds look more like an adult in overall plumage.

Breeding-plumaged adults have a pale gray mantle and white otherwise. The bill is bright yellow with a black band and the legs are also yellow. In the winter they have brown streaking on the head.

Black Tern

Childonias niger

L 9.5″ | **WS** 23″

The breeding plumaged Black Tern stands out from other terns with its exquisite black head and body and slaty-gray upperparts and wings. The only other terns that have predominantly dark body plumage are rare and found only out in the Gulf of Mexico. They are uncommon to abundant migrants throughout the state on their way to and from the coasts of central and northern South America. These small terns can be found on beaches, tidal flats, freshwater wetlands, and even over agricultural fields and pastures. An uncommon to common migrant throughout the state and these birds congregate in large numbers along the coast before continuing their migration. Migrants pass through the state between mid-March and May and from July through October.

They have dark plumage overall with a thin, black bill in breeding plumage.

Winter plumaged birds are gray above with dark crown, ear patch, and a "spur" on side of breast.

Forster's Tern

Sterna forsteri

L 13.5" | **WS** 31"

The Forster's Tern is the most widespread tern found in Texas. There are two distinct breeding areas in North America. The majority of the population breeds across southern Canada and the northern United States, but they are also common breeders along the western Gulf Coast. They are one of a group of medium-size terns that are very similar in appearance. The only other one that is of regular occurrence in Texas is Common Tern (*Sterna hirundo*). Forster's Terns can be found over both salt and freshwater habitats where they feed over open water by diving for food. They are common permanent residents along the coast and common to uncommon migrant through all areas of the state. Migrants are found state between March and May and from August through October.

Adults in summer plumage have pale gray upperparts with a deeply forked tail. The bill is orange with a black tip.

In winter, they are white with pale gray upperparts and pale wingtips. The head is largely white with a large black patch over the eye. They have orange legs and feet and the bill is mostly dark.

Royal Tern

Thalasseus maximus

L 17.7–19.6″ | **WS** 49.2–53.1″

There are two large terns that can be found on the Texas coast; the Royal and Caspian Terns (*Hydroprogne caspia*). The Royal Tern is the sleeker of the two with the Caspian Tern being much bulkier and bigger headed with a redder bill. Like some other terns, the Royal Tern is in full breeding plumage for a rather short period of time and it is not uncommon to see birds in a non-breeding plumage throughout the spring and summer. They are common permanent residents along the immediate coast and are rarely encountered more than a few miles inland. There are a few such records including birds that wandered as far inland as the Dallas area and the western Trans-Pecos often in association with tropical storms and hurricanes.

Breeding plumaged birds have a black forehead and crown and the bill is bright orange.

Black crested in all plumages with pale gray upperparts and white underparts. The bill is orange which varies in intensity through the year. Non-breeding adults and juveniles have a white forehead and crown.

Sandwich Tern

Thalasseus sandvicensis

L 13.3–17.7″ | **WS** 33–35.4″

The Sandwich Tern is slender with a long bill and a short crest. They are virtually restricted to saltwater habitats along the coast. All inland occurrences in Texas are associated with hurricanes or tropical storms. Sandwich Terns are common summer residents becoming rare to uncommon in winter.

Breeding plumaged birds have a black forehead and crown that includes a short crest. The bill is black with a yellow tip in adults and entirely black in immature birds. They are white with pale gray upperparts.

In non-breeding plumage they have a white forehead and crown, but retain the yellow tip on the otherwise black bill. This yellow tip can sometimes be hard to see against a bright sky.

Black Skimmer

Rynchops niger

L 15.7–19.6″ | **WS** 45.2″

Seeing a Black Skimmer feed is a real treat. They fly just above the water's surface pushing the knife-thin lower part of the bill through the water. It is extremely sensitive and they are able to close their bill in an instant when they find prey. They are unique among North American birds in that the lower half of the bill is notably longer than the upper part. These birds are restricted to coastal habitats and are very rarely found inland with inland records most often associated with tropical storms. They are locally common along the entire coast.

Adults in breeding plumage have black upperparts that include the upper half of the head. The bill is red with a black tip.

In the winter they develop a white collar. Juveniles are brownish above often heavily speckled with white.

Rock Pigeon

Columba livia

L 13″ | **WS** 23″

The Rock Pigeon is one of the very widespread birds that have been introduced to North America from Europe. First released in Nova Scotia in the early 1600s, they reached Texas in the early 1900s. These birds are common to abundant permanent residents in urban areas and rare to uncommon in more rural habitats. They use man-made structures for nesting habitat that mimics the cliffs used by the native population. An effect of long domestication is the tremendous variability in plumage as well as some of the odd feather adornments that have been selected for in captive breeding.

The plumage of the natural population is pale gray with a white rump and two bold black bars on wings. The head and neck are darker gray and a darker band across the tip of the tail.

Eurasian Collared-Dove

Streptopelia decaocto

L 11.5-11.75" | **WS** 18.5-21.6"

The rapid colonization of the Eurasian Collard-Dove in Texas borders on the unbelievable. A relatively small number was released in 1974 in the Bahamas and made their way to Florida within a few years. The first occurrence of birds thought to originate from this population reached Texas in 1994 and by 2000 they could be found in virtually every town in the state. Since then, they have spread all the way to California and north to Alaska. Uncommon to abundant permanent residents in urban areas, they can also be found around human habitats in rural areas as well. They are rare in natural habitats and are generally not found in forests. Coloration varies considerably ranging from nearly white to the more typical grayish-brown.

A large dove with grayish-brown plumage and a black line on the hind neck in adults. The primaries are blackish contrasting with the rest of the wing.

White-winged Dove

Zenaida asiatica

L 11–12″ | **WS** 19.2–20.4″

White-winged Doves have undergone a tremendous range expansion over the past forty years. They were originally a bird that was restricted to the Lower Rio Grande Valley and along the Rio Grande in the Trans-Pecos. Starting in the 1970s, however, they began colonizing areas to the north, particularly cities. They are now found in virtually all areas of the state except the pine forests of East Texas. They are even more common in urban areas, such as San Antonio, than they were in their original range. These birds are common to abundant permanent residents throughout the southern half of the state and northward to the Dallas-Fort Worth area, becoming uncommon and local in urban habits on the South Plains and north through the Panhandle. Their familiar, four-note call is *Who cooks for you?*

They are stocky with light brown plumage. They have a bold white stripe along the base of the flight feathers that shows well even at rest. The tail has a broad white band across the tip.

Mourning Dove

Zenaida macroura

L 11″ | **WS** 14.5–17.5″

The Mourning Dove is reported to be the most common game bird in North America. They seem to be much more uncommon in urban habitats now with this change often blamed on the increased competition with more aggressive Eurasian Collared and White-winged Doves. Mourning Doves are common to abundant permanent residents in natural habitats throughout Texas. There is considerable migration within the population with birds from the north moving into the state for the winter and some of the breeding birds migrating farther south.

They are slender with brown plumage and a long, pointed tail.

Inca Dove

Columbina inca

L 7–9″ | **WS** 11.4″

Like the White-winged Dove, the Inca Dove has undergone an impressive northward range expansion into Texas. In the 1880s, these small doves were known only from the Lower Rio Grande Valley, but by 1904 they were being found as far north as Waco. This expansion ultimately included all of the state north to Lubbock and Amarillo. This trend has been reversed in recent years as the northern edge of their range appears to be retreating. Inca Doves are common permanent residents in the southern two-thirds of the state and uncommon to rare farther north.

The body plumage of these dove is edged with black giving them a distinctly scaled appearance. They tail is long and edged in white and the primaries are rufous.

Yellow-billed Cuckoo

Coccyzus americanus

L 11″ | **WS** 16″

The Yellow-billed Cuckoo is rather secretive in its habits and is more often heard than seen. These birds have two types of calls, one is a rapid series of *kuk* notes that slows down and descends into an extended *kakakpwlp,* while the other is a slow series of *coo* notes. They are uncommon migrants and summer residents in Texas. Overall the population of Yellow-billed Cuckoos is declining, but that trend is much more pronounced in the birds of the western United States which includes the Trans-Pecos of Texas. They are found in forest and woodland habitats which are restricted primarily to riparian corridors in the West. These two populations differ in their timing of occurrence with birds in the East arriving in the spring early April while the western birds do not reach the state until mid-May. Fall migration is from mid-August to mid-October.

They are slender with brown upperparts and are white below. In flight, the primaries are rufous and each tail feather has a large white tip. The bill is mostly yellow and slightly down curved.

Greater Roadrunner

Geococcyx californianus

L 20.5-21.5″ | **WS** 19.5″

The Greater Roadrunner is perhaps the bird most associated with the southwestern deserts. They are actually common permanent residents throughout much of the state and with land-use changes in the forests of east Texas they have become uncommon and local even there. Males are very territorial and will defend the same area for years. Although capable fliers, they spend most of the time on the ground including running down lizards, snakes, and small mammals for food.

Slender bodied with a long graduated tail that is often held cocked upward. The upperparts and breast are iridescent green with buffy mottling. The belly is grayish-white. A patch of bare skin behind the eye is red and blue during breeding season and often gray otherwise. As with other cuckoos, their feet are zygodactyl with two toes pointing forward and two backward.

Groove-billed Ani

Crotophaga sulcirostris

L 13.3″ | **WS** 16″

The Groove-billed Ani is a tropical bird that reaches the northern extent of its range in the brush country of South Texas. These odd birds are somewhat secretive and never far from dense cover. They are also often seen in small flocks, even at the height of nesting season. This is because they are cooperative nesters with non-breeding "helpers" taking part in incubation and care for the young. Groove-billed Anis are common summer residents in the Lower Rio Grande Valley and uncommon farther north through the South Texas Brush Country. Most migrant south by October and return in late April. A few can be found in the winter and are more common close to the coast during that season.

They are black overall with overtones of iridescent purple and green. The tail is long and often wagged as if it were not well attached. The bill is thick and at close range grooves can be seen.

Barn Owl

Tyto alba

L 14" | **WS** 39.5–49"

The Barn Owl is one of the few species of birds that is found on every continent except Antarctica. However, they barely occur in Canada and their distribution in Asia is limited to the far south. They are more common in open habitats ranging from open grassland to woodland. Often nesting in cavities these birds will take advantage of man-made structures and readily use barns and other buildings as nesting sites. A rare to locally uncommon permanent resident throughout most of the state they tend to be very local in the forested areas of east Texas.

A slender owl that is largely white below and yellowish-brown above. There is dark spotting on the underparts which varied greatly. They have dark eyes in a heart-shape face.

Eastern Screech-Owl

Megascops asio

L 8.5″ | **WS** 20″

There are two species of screech-owls found in Texas. The more common and widespread of these is the Eastern Screech-Owl. They are common permanent residents through the eastern two-thirds of the state and are found in forest and woodland habitats, including within cities where large trees are present. In the westernmost part of their range they are more restricted to riparian corridors. As they are strictly nocturnal, their small size allows them to go undetected unless their distinctive calls are heard. They have a quivering whinny as well as a series of hoots. They will also readily use nest boxes.

A small owl with yellow eyes. Most of the Texas birds are gray with heavily streaked and barred underparts. There are red morph birds as well with those being most common in the eastern third of the state.

Great Horned Owl

Bubo virginianus

L 21.5″ | **WS** 40–57″

The Great Horned Owl is probably the most familiar of the owls that occurs in Texas. Quite vocal and active at dusk and dawn, these owls are much more likely to be seen than some of the other species that are also common in the state. They are a powerful owl and fierce hunter and have been known to take large prey such as skunks and raccoons. Birds that are roosting on an open perch are also viable prey. Nesting starts early in the year, often as early as January, and they will use nests built by hawks or ravens. They are common permanent residents throughout the state except in the Pineywoods of East Texas where they are uncommon.

Large with prominent ear tufts and yellow eyes. Mottled brown above and heavily barred below with a conspicuous white patch on the throat.

Barred Owl

Strix varia

L 20″ | **WS** 42″

The Barred Owl is the forest owl of the eastern half of Texas, where they are generally uncommon to common permanent residents. Not strictly nocturnal, these owls can be active during the day and feed on a wide variety of prey, including birds, small mammals, and reptiles. This includes Eastern Screech-Owl which they find by homing in on their calls. The call of the Barred Owl is well-known within its range as it is loud and far reaching. They most often give a call that sounds like *Who cooks for you, who cooks for you all?* However, they make a bewildering assortment of calls.

They have dark eyes and a rounded head with grayish-brown upperparts heavily spotted with white. Below they are pale gray and heavily barred on the breast and streaked on the belly.

Elf Owl

Micrathene whitneyi

L 4.8–5.5″ | **WS** 14.9″

The Elf Owl is the smallest owl found in the United States and is most often associated with the southwestern deserts. In Texas, they are uncommon to locally common summer residents in the southern Trans-Pecos eastward to the southwestern Hill Country and in the Lower Rio Grande Valley. They feed primarily on insects and other arthropods and are occasionally drawn to security lights in search of food. The most frequently given call is a series of short, whistled yelping notes. They also give a single downward inflected bark-like call.

They are tiny with a very round head and long legs. The upperparts are gray with flecks of rufous and brown. The underparts are pale gray and heavily streaked with rufous, brown and gray. The face generally has more rufous feathers and the eyes are yellow.

Burrowing Owl

Athene cunicularia

L 7.5–8″ | **WS** 21.5″

Burrowing Owls, as the name implies, use burrows for nesting sites. On the Great Plains they are very often associated with prairie-dogs. In addition, they have adapted to use small culverts and other man-made underground cavities as roosting and nesting sites. They are locally common summer residents in the Panhandle and South Plains becoming uncommon to rare south into the Trans-Pecos. Typically, uncommon within this range in the winter they can be found throughout the western two-thirds of the state during that season. There have been unexpected nesting records from well outside of the breeding range including one from Kenedy County. Migrants and winter residents can be found from mid-September through April.

Long-legged with a round head and yellow eyes. They have brown upperparts with a brown breast that is spotted with white that gives way to a white belly with brown barring.

Common Nighthawk

Chordeiles minor

L 9″ | **WS** 21.5″

Common Nighthawks are very active at dusk and dawn as they hunt for flying insects. They are agile fliers with long wings and frequently give a single *peent* call while on the wing. Common Nighthawks are uncommon to common migrants and summer residents in open habitats throughout the state except in the forested regions of East Texas. During the day they roost on the ground, on tree limbs, fence posts, roof tops, and other flat surfaces. The overall population has been declining in recent decades and is a species of conservation concern. Migrants and summer residents can be found from April through October.

During the day they are often found on the ground or fairly close to the ground. They are generally mottled black, brown, and white above and barred below, but there is considerable variation in color.

In flight, they have long, pointed wings with a bold white band across the primaries. They have a very large mouth and short bill.

Common Pauraque

Nyctidromus albicollis

L 11–11.8″ | **WS** 24.8″

The Common Pauraque is a large nightjar that is found throughout the neotropics and reaches the northern point in its distribution in southern Texas. These birds are particularly active just after dusk and before dawn. They are common permanent residents in the South Texas Brush Country and their range appears to be slowly inching northward. Roost sites are on the ground where a dense overstory of shrubs is present while feeding areas are most often in nearby clearings. The most frequent call is a descending *wheeer* but they have a low pur call as well.

They are large with a notably long tail. The head is large with an obvious rufous cheek when seen in good light. The body plumage is quite intricate with rufous, browns, tans and blacks mixed. They roost on the ground and most often sit on the ground during feeding bouts.

Common Poorwill

Phalaenoptilus nuttallii

L 7.4–8.2" | **WS** 17.3"

The Common Poorwill is a small nightjar of the western half of the state. They are found in open habitats ranging from desert to open grassland. During the spring and early summer these birds call incessantly just after dusk and before dawn. An interesting aspect of their natural history is the ability to enter a state of torpor in the winter and only become active when the evening temperatures are above normal allowing for insects to be more active. They are common to rare summer residents throughout the western half of the state. Their actual status in the winter is hard to determine, but they have been found in the southern Trans-Pecos and South Texas Brush Country. The common name is derived from the call, a whistled *poor-will*.

These small nightjars normally roost on the ground. They have large heads and large eyes. The tail is short and broadly tipped in white in males and more narrowly so in females.

Chuck-will's-widow

Antrostomus carolinensis

L 11–12.5" | **WS** 22.8–24"

The Chuck-will's-widow is very well known for its emphatic calling after dark. These large nightjars get their common name from their song. They are found in forest and woodland habitats with an understory of shrubs where they primarily roost on the ground. They are uncommon to common migrants and summer resident through the eastern half of the state. This species is often confused with the Whip-poor-will (*Caprimulgus vociferous*) because of the wider public knowledge of that closely related species.

A large nightjar with a long tail. Like other nightjars, they have large heads and eyes. Most are primarily rufous in color, but they do vary and a few are grayish. The male has white on the inner webbing of the outer tail feathers.

Chimney Swift

Chaetura pelagica

L 5.25″ | **WS** 11″

The Chimney Swift is the swift of eastern North America. They spend the vast majority of their time in flight, landing only at the nest or to roost. This bird is a common migrant and summer resident over the eastern two-thirds of the state and the only swift likely to be seen in Texas outside of the Trans-Pecos region. These birds have adapted to human infrastructure and now nest most frequently in unused chimneys and smoke stacks. This habit has given rise to the development of swift towers that can provide a nesting and roosting location. These birds are often seen in small groups, especially after the young leave the nest. They are very vocal giving a *chip* call in a rapid series. Migrants and summer residents can be found between March and October.

Reminiscent of a cigar with wings. They have long wings and a short, almost unnoticeable tail. The plumage is grayish-brown and they have a slightly paler throat. They are acrobatic in flight and can seem erratic as they chase flying insects.

White-throated Swift

Aeronautes saxatalis

L 5.9–7″ | **WS** 13.3″

Found in the Trans-Pecos, this swift is much less obvious than the Chimney Swift of the East. These birds roost and nest in crevices on cliff faces and often feed very high in the sky. They are colonial breeders and near nesting sites are very vocal giving a high pitched *sheeee* or *kee-kee-kee* call. These acrobatic fliers are often seen in large groups and are common summer residents in the Trans-Pecos eastward to the western edge of the Hill Country becoming uncommon in winter when part of the population migrates south.

Long, narrow wings with a slightly forked tail.

Lucifer Hummingbird

Calothorax lucifer

L 3.5″ | **WS** 4″

The Lucifer Hummingbird is found almost exclusively in Mexico and just reaches the United States in southeastern Arizona and the southern Trans-Pecos of Texas. They are locally common summer residents in the foothills of the Chisos and Christmas Mountains. There is a regular post-breeding movement north into the Davis Mountains as well. Lucifer means "the torchbearer" and presumably refers to the purple gorget of the male. These, along with the Black-chinned Hummingbird, are the only species found in the desert foothills in the early summer and both are attracted to the flower stalks of century plants. Spring migrants reach the breeding grounds in early March and most of the population has left by early October.

These small hummingbirds have a notably down curved bill. In adult males the gorget is purple, the corners of which extend down the neck. The tail in long and deeply forked, but this feature is often not apparent on perched birds.

Adult females have a buffy wash over their underparts. There is also a post ocular stripe that widens down the side of the neck.

Ruby-throated Hummingbird

Archilochus colubris

L 3–3.5″ | **WS** 3–4.5″

The only commonly occurring hummingbird in the eastern half of the United States is the Ruby-throated Hummingbird. In Texas they are common summer residents east of the Hill Country. During spring migration they are found westward through the eastern Hill Country and Rolling Plains, but in fall they are found as far west as the Davis Mountains where they are generally rare but some years are fairly common. Although some of the population migrates straight across the Gulf of Mexico, many go around it. There can be many thousands in the woodlands close to the immediate coast in September. Overall they are found from early March through October.

The males are emerald green above with green flanks. They have a deep red gorget that is bordered below by white. The throat can look black except when sunlight hits it just at the right angle. The tail is obviously, but shallowly, forked.

Adult females have whitish throats and underparts. They are green above and that includes the crown. The tail has broad white tips on the outer feathers.

Black-chinned Hummingbird

Archilochus alexandri

L 3.7 WS 4.3"

The Black-chinned Hummingbird is a close cousin of the Ruby-throated Hummingbird. These birds are summer residents throughout the western half of the state. The range of the Black-chinned starts where the Ruby-throated leaves off on the eastern edge of the Hill Country. There are instances of hybridization between these species, but for the most part they nest in separate areas. Black-chinned Hummingbirds can be seen through the western two-thirds of Texas during migration. They are present in the state between late February and September.

Adult males are green above and grayish below with a black throat that is bordered below by a narrow purplish gorget. The purple can only be seen in direct sunlight.

Adult females are similar to the Ruby-throated, but are grayer overall and particularly on the crown.

Broad-tailed Hummingbird

Selasphorus platycercus

L 3.2–3.8″ | **WS** 5.1″

The Broad-tailed Hummingbird is a bird of the Mountain West. They are summer residents found in the Rocky Mountains from southern Idaho southward, including the highest mountains ranges of the Trans-Pecos. The males have a notch in one of their primaries that makes a high pitched whistle when in flight. This sound is often the first clue that one is nearby. Broad-tailed Hummingbirds have a rose-red gorget and as a result are often mistaken for the more well-known Ruby-throated Hummingbird. Broad-tailed Hummingbirds are common to uncommon migrants through the western third of Texas and increasingly rare farther east.

The males have a pinkish-red gorget. They are bright green above with green flanks and white underparts.

Adult females have whitish throats that are often heavily spotted with green. The upperparts are green and the flanks are obviously buffy.

Rufous Hummingbird

Selasphorus rufus

L 2.75-3.5" | **WS** 4.5"

The male Rufous Hummingbird is one of the more spectacular hummingbirds in the United States. Their bright rufous coloration is reminiscent of a new penny. They are also the hummingbird that nests the farthest north on the continent with the northern extent of the range in southern Alaska. Rufous Hummingbirds are a common to abundant fall migrant through the western half of the state and are rare, but annual farther east. In the spring they are very rare as the majority of the population migrates northward up the west coast of North America. These birds are very hardy and will spend the winter almost anywhere in the state, although they are most common on the coastal prairies. Migrants pass through between early July and October.

The male is bright rufous overall with some white on the breast and down the belly. They have a green crown and varying amounts of green speckles on the back.

Adult females are green above and have buffy-rufous flanks. They also have a triangle of iridescent orange feathers at the base of the throat. Immature males resemble the females, but have rufous feathering on the lower back and rump.

Buff-bellied Hummingbird

Amazilia yucatanensis

L 3.9–4.3″ | **WS** 5.5″

The Buff-bellied Hummingbird is a tropical hummingbird that is found primarily in eastern Mexico from the Yucatan Peninsula northward into southern Texas. They are part of a very large assemblage of hummingbirds that are largely iridescent green in their body plumage and have red at the base of their bills. Buff-bellied Hummingbirds are uncommon to locally common summer residents from the Lower Rio Grande Valley northward along the coast to Victoria. They are expanding their range northward and are now found sporadically northward to Bastrop and even the southwestern Pineywoods. In the winter most of the population leaves, but a small number actually move northward up the coastal prairies.

The males and females look alike with bright green upperparts and buffy colored bellies. The throat is iridescent green and the tail is dark rufous. The bill is red at the base, but the extent of the color varies.

Ringed Kingfisher

Megaceryle torquatus

L 11–14″ | **WS** 20–23″

The spectacular Ringed Kingfisher is a tropical bird that's range reaches the United States in Texas. They are large kingfishers, easily dwarfing the more common and widespread Belted Kingfisher. Ringed Kingfishers began to occur in Texas with greater regularity in the 1950s and the first nest was discovered in 1970. Since then, they have steadily moved northward and are now found throughout South Texas and along all of the major rivers in the Hill Country. They are locally common in the Lower Rio Grande Valley and uncommon and local farther north.

They are large-headed birds with a bushy crest and a large bill. The males are blue-gray above and rufous below with a bright white throat. Females are very similar, but have a blue-gray chest.

Belted Kingfisher

Megaceryle alcyon

L 12.5" | **WS** 21"

The Belted Kingfisher is by far the most common and widespread kingfisher found in Texas. As the name implies, kingfishers are extraordinarily adept at capturing fish, their primary food. These birds capture fish by diving headfirst into the water before emerging and flying to a nearby perch. Belted Kingfishers are solitary birds except during the breeding season where they nest in burrows, which they dig in earthen banks, and this behavior is a limiting factor on potential nesting locations. They are very vocal, especially in flight when they give a loud rattle call. These birds are uncommon to locally common winter residents throughout the state and uncommon and local in summer in the northern third. Migrants and winter residents are present from mid-August through April

They are large-headed birds with a bushy crest and a large bill. The head and upperparts are blue-gray contrasting with the white underparts. Males have a blue-gray breast band that can be flecked with brown or rusty feathers.

Females look virtually identical to males with the exception of a rusty belly band below breast band.

Green Kingfisher

Chloroceryle americana

L 8.6–11.8″ | **WS** 11.5–12.0″

The diminutive Green Kingfisher is another tropical bird that also occurs in Texas. These small kingfishers are found on quiet streams and prefer areas with clear water. The have a longer bill by proportion than the other kingfishers found in Texas. They often sit on perches close to the surface of the water to watch for fish and are fairly vocal, often giving a repeated *tick* call. An uncommon resident throughout South Texas and northward into the Hill Country with the northern edge of the range varying considerably depending on the severity of the winter.

As the name suggests, they are green above and white below. Males have a broad rufous chest band.

Females look very similar to the males but have two partial bands across the underparts. They often have a buffy wash of color on the white of the face and throat.

Red-headed Woodpecker

Melanerpes erythrocephalus

L 7.5–9.25″ | **WS** 17″

An adult Red-headed Woodpecker is one of the most striking birds that occur in Texas. They are locally common permanent residents in the Pineywoods of East Texas. Farther west, they are uncommon to rare in riparian woodland across the northern third of the state to the eastern Panhandle. Away from the Pineywoods these woodpeckers have been declining over the past forty years. Interestingly, the large scale demise of trees because of the severe drought from 2011 through 2013 has provided abundant foraging habitat and as a result Red-headed Woodpeckers have been found in greater numbers in the Oaks and Prairies region than during the past twenty years.

The entirely red head of the adult is unique among Texas woodpeckers. They have black upperparts and are white below. The wings are largely black with large white patches.

Immature birds have a gray head and upperparts as well as bars through the white wing patches.

Golden-fronted Woodpecker

Melanerpes aurifrons

L 8.75-10.25" | **WS** 16.9"

The Golden-fronted Woodpecker is almost a Texas specialty in the United States. They do occur in southwestern Oklahoma, but the majority of their range is in Mexico. These woodpeckers occur in open woodland including the extensive honey mesquite found on the Rolling Plains. A common permanent resident from the southeastern Panhandle south through the Rolling Plains to the Lower Rio Grande Valley, in the southern Trans-Pecos, they are uncommon in riparian habitats. Golden-fronted refers to the golden coloring on the forehead.

In addition to the golden-yellow forehead, the adult male has a red cap and an orange nape. The upperparts are barred black and white and the underparts and face are tan. Adult males also have a golden-yellow wash on the belly that is not always easy to see.

The female is very similar to the male, but lacks the bright red cap.

Red-bellied Woodpecker

Melanerpes carolinus

L 9.25" | **WS** 16"

The Red-bellied Woodpecker is the eastern counterpart to the Golden-fronted Woodpecker. They are found in the open woodland in the eastern third of the state and in the eastern Panhandle. Their range overlaps that of the Golden-fronted only in the eastern Hill Country, but in this region the Red-bellied is restricted to riparian woodland. They are common to abundant in most of their range in Texas and are one of the more frequently encountered woodpeckers in urban areas. Although generally inconspicuous, they have a reddish wash on the lower belly. This coloration is brightest when the feathers are new and is slowly worn off as the feathers are abraded, especially during nesting.

The adult male has a bright red crown and nape. The upperparts are zebra striped and the underparts and face are tan. There is an inconspicuous red patch on the lower belly.

The female is very similar, but the red on the head is restricted to the nape.

Yellow-bellied Sapsucker

Sphyrapicus varius

L 7–8.75" | **WS** 13.5–16"

Sapsuckers are well known for drilling rows of shallow holes in the trunks of trees. These holes ooze sap and attract insects and these woodpeckers feed on both. Although all four species of sapsuckers have been found in Texas, the Yellow-bellied Sapsucker is by far the most common and widespread. They are uncommon to locally common migrants and winter residents throughout the eastern three-quarters of the state. In the eastern Trans-Pecos they are rare to locally uncommon. They do not nest in Texas. Migrants and winter residents are found in Texas from October to March with a few lingering well into April.

In adult males the head is largely black with two prominent white stripes and red on the forehead and throat. The back is heavily mottled with black and white contrasting with the solid black wings. There is a prominent white stripe on the wings that is normally visible even when perched. The underparts are yellow, although the brightness varies considerably.

The females are similar but have a white throat.

Ladder-backed Woodpecker

Dryobates scalaris

L 6.25–7″ | **WS** 12.9″

The most common woodpecker in the western two-thirds of Texas is the diminutive Ladder-backed Woodpecker. They are often thought of as birds of the desert that feed on ocotillo or cholla, but they can be found in a wide variety of habitats. This bird is the most common woodpecker of the oak-juniper woodland of the Hill Country and the mesquite woodland of the Rolling Plains. Ladder-backed Woodpeckers are found east through the western half of the Oaks and Prairies region and seen to be expanding their range eastward up the coastal prairies. They are very vocal and the descending whinny sounds as if they are laughing.

As the name implies, they have a zebra stripped back and the black wings are very heavily spotted with white which expands the look. The head is mainly white with two prominent black stripes and in males, a red crown that extends into the upper nape. The underparts are whitish and heavily spotted with black.

The female is nearly identical to the male, but lacks the red on the head.

Downy Woodpecker

Dryobates pubescens

L 6″ | **WS** 11″

The Downy Woodpecker is the smallest woodpecker found in North America. This small size allows it to feed on small branches and even weed stalks that are not easily accessible by large woodpeckers. They are common to uncommon permanent residents east of the Rolling Plains and Hill Country. They can also be found in riparian areas along the large rivers in the eastern Hill Country and in the eastern Panhandle. Downy Woodpeckers are rare winter visitors west through the remainder of the Hill Country and northward and are normally seen between November and March.

Their small size is usually quite evident as is their very small and stubby bill. They have a white back and black wings with extensive white spotting. The head is striped with black and white. The outer tail feathers are white with black spots. Adult males have small red patch on white hind crown.

Red-cockaded Woodpecker

Dryobates borealis

L 8–9" | **WS** 14"

Listed as an Endangered Species, the Red-cockaded Woodpecker is a specialist of open pine forests. These birds depend on healthy stands of mature pines that are maintained using fire. These forests have a savannah-like appearance and lack a heavy understory of woody shrubs. The population in Sam Houston National Forest is one of the largest remaining. These birds are much less solitary than most woodpeckers and remain in family groups for much of the year. Red-cockaded Woodpeckers nest in live pines, where they drill small holes around the nest entrance that causes the area to become caked with pine resin. Overall they are rare to locally uncommon.

They are black and white overall with a large white cheek patch. The upperparts are black and heavily marked with white and the underparts are white with some black speckling. The adult male has a very small area of red feathers on top of the white cheek, but is rarely seen.

Northern Flicker

Colaptes auratus

L 11.5″ | **WS** 18″

The Northern Flicker is one of the more colorful woodpeckers found in Texas. They have either orange-red or yellow coloration on the underside of the wing and tail feathers. Northern Flickers spend a lot of time foraging on the ground eating ants and other insectes. The two distinctive populations were formerly considered separate species. The birds in the East were known as "Yellow-shafted Flickers" and they are common to uncommon permanent residents in the Pineywoods and west across the northern third of the state. In winter they can be found through the eastern three-quarters of the state. The western "Red-shafted Flicker" is an uncommon nester in the highest mountains of the Trans-Pecos and is uncommon through the western half of the state in winter.

They have brown backs that are barred with black. Yellow-shafted birds have a tan face and a gray crown and nape with a red nape patch. There is a black crescent on breast and the whitish underparts are spotted with black. The undersides of the wing and tail feathers are bright yellow. Adult males have a black "whisker."

Red-shafted birds are similar in coloration with red on the underside of the wing and tail feathers. The face on these birds is gray and they have a brown crown and nape. Adult males have a red "whisker."

Pileated Woodpecker

Dryocopus pileatus

L 17.5″ | **WS** 27.5″

By far the largest woodpecker found in Texas is the crow-sized Pileated Woodpecker. Their large size and black-and-white coloration has led to these birds being misidentified as the probably extinct Ivory-billed Woodpecker (*Campephilus principalis*). The very loud *cuk-cuk-cuk-cuk* call of the Pileated Woodpecker is often the first indication that the bird is present. Pileated Woodpeckers often forage on the ground and on downed logs. They are uncommon to locally uncommon permanent residents through the Pineywoods and westward through the Oaks and Prairies region.

They have a black body with a white face striped with black. Adult males have a red "whisker" and crest, the red is only on the crest in females. In flight, a white stripe on the neck extends down to the white underwings.

Crested Caracara

Caracara cheriway

L 19.2–22.8″ | **WS** 47.2″

The Crested Caracara is a common sight along the roadsides of the South Texas Brush Country. These large birds are related to falcons, but frequently take advantage of roadkills for a meal. Their very long legs allow them to stalk the ground looking for prey and, as such they are frequently observed in grassy fields. Crested Caracara is the national bird of Mexico and is frequently referred to in Texas as a "Mexican Eagle." They are uncommon to common permanent residents in South Texas and northward up the coastal prairies west of Galveston Bay, including on the barrier islands. They are uncommon farther north up the Oaks and Prairies region and in the Hill Country.

These long-legged falcons have a white head with a black crest and orange-red bare skin on the face. They have a wide white collar that is barred below before blending into the black belly. The tail is white with a broad black band across the tip. The primaries are also white.

American Kestrel

Falco sparverius

L 10.5″ | **WS** 22″

The smallest falcon found in Texas is the American Kestrel. These very colorful birds are also by far the most common falcon in the state. They are probably most frequently seen on overhead lines in rural areas, but they are also well adapted to living in more urban environments as well. Kestrels feed on everything from large insects to small rodents. American Kestrels are uncommon and local summer residents in the Panhandle south through the northern half of the Trans-Pecos and east to the Dallas-Fort Worth area. They are also found in summer in South Texas and in the Pineywoods. They are common to abundant winter residents in all parts of the state. Migrants and winter residents can be found between September and April.

The adult male is a very colorful falcon with long slaty gray wings and rufous tail. The back is rusty in color and the underparts are washed with a rich orange-buff. The face is marked with black vertical bars.

Adult females are rusty above and heavily barred. The rusty tail is also heavily barred and the underparts are heavily streaked with rufous-brown.

Peregrine Falcon

Falco peregrinus

L 16.5″ | **WS** 41″

The Peregrine Falcon is one of the great conservation success stories. It has dramatically recovered from very low population levels in the 1970s because of the effects of the pesticide DDT. The side effect on birds of DDT was the thinning of eggs shells making successful nesting rare. Peregrines are now uncommon to rare migrants throughout the state and are local nesters in the canyons of the Big Bend region. In winter, they are locally uncommon along the coastal prairies and are frequently seen on or near beaches. Migrants and winter residents can be found from September through April.

Adults are bluish-gray above and pale below and heavily barred. The head has a helmeted look with long "sideburn" extending down through the face. In immature birds the blue color is replaced with brown.

Red-crowned Parrot

Amazona viridigenalis

L 12″ | **WS** 25″

The Red-crowned Parrot is primarily found in northeastern Mexico where they are critically endangered. Their numbers have declined due to habitat loss and young taken for the pet trade. They were first noted in Texas in 1970s and some of the population may have arrived as a result of displacement because of habitat loss. They are now common in urban areas in the Lower Rio Grande Valley with flocks containing up to 300 birds found in the winter. The Texas population is probably made up largely of descendants of escaped or released cage birds, but that does not lessen their importance for the continuing existence of the species. They are very loud, often making raucous calls that can be heard from a great distance.

They are green overall with rounded wings and a short tail. They have a red forehead and crown and red secondaries.

Olive-sided Flycatcher

Contopus cooperi

L 7–8" | **WS** 12.9"

The Olive-sided Flycatcher is a member of mostly olive-colored flycatchers that are often difficult to identify. These birds have an upright posture and frequently choose exposed perches in the tops of trees. They will sally out from the perch chasing insects and very often return to the same spot. They are uncommon to rare migrants throughout the state. Spring migrants can be found between late April and early June and fall migrants from early August through October.

Medium-size flycatchers with brownish-olive upperparts, including the head. The underparts have a strongly "vested" look with olive flanks with bright white on the throat and extending through the middle of the breast to the tail. The white extends around the body on the lower flanks and can often be seen as spots above the folded wing when perched.

Western Wood-Pewee

Contopus sordidulus

L 5.5–6.25" | **WS** 10"

There are two species of wood-pewees that occur in Texas and other than by voice they can be impossible to tell apart. The Western Wood-Pewee occurs primarily in the western half of the state. These flycatchers have an erect perching posture and often return to the same perch when hawking for insects. The Western Wood-Pewee is a common to uncommon migrant through the western third of the state and a locally uncommon nesting bird in the Davis and Guadalupe Mountains. Migrants can be found between late April and early June and from August through October. The call is a slightly descending *peeer* in contrast to the clear *peWEE* of the Eastern Wood-Pewee (*Contopus virens*).

Grayish-brown overall with two thin, white wing bars. They lack a prominent eye ring and the lower mandible is orange-yellow at least at the base. The underparts are slightly paler with grayish "vest" across breast. Western Wood-Pewees are generally darker, but identification is best by voice and to a lesser extent, range.

Least Flycatcher

Empidonax minimus

L 5.25" | **WS** 7.75"

There is a group of small flycatchers that are very similar in appearance and all belong to the genus *Empidonax*. They are often referred to as Empids and one or more of these birds can be found in all areas of the state. One of the most common members of this group is the Least Flycatcher. They are common to uncommon migrants through the eastern three-quarters of Texas. They do not nest in Texas, but are very rare winter residents in the Lower Rio Grande Valley and along the coast. Migrants are seen from mid-April to early June and from late July through October.

Brownish-olive above with two bold whitish wing bars. They have a prominent eye ring that is white and round. The underparts mostly pale, but usually have a wash of gray on the flanks.

Black Phoebe

Sayornis nigricans

L 6.25" | **WS** 11"

The Black Phoebe is a bird that is almost always found in close association with water, particularly flowing streams and small rivers, but they are also at home around ponds. They are very often seen perched on rock or branches just above the surface of the water. Black Phoebes are locally common permanent residents in the Trans-Pecos, the western Hill Country, and south through the western South Texas Brush Country.

Sooty-black overall with the exception of a white belly. The head is slightly darker than the back.

Eastern Phoebe

Sayornis phoebe

L 5.5–6.5" | **WS** 10–11"

The Eastern Phoebe has adapted well to human activity and frequently nests under bridges and eves of houses. Rather drab in coloration which may cause some confusion with other flycatchers, the Eastern Phoebe has a distinct habit of frequently dipping its tail downward when perched. This behavior is not shared by any other brown-colored flycatcher. They are uncommon to common nesting birds in the northern half of the state starting in the eastern Panhandle south through the Hill Country. As migrants they can be found throughout the state and in winter they can be found throughout to the eastern Trans-Pecos. The common name is a reflection of its song, *fee-bee,* which can be heard even in the middle of winter.

The upperparts are brown and contrast with the darker brown head. The underparts are pale with a wide brown wash on the flanks. They lack an eyeing and only immature birds have prominent wing bars.

Say's Phoebe

Sayornis saya

L 6.76" | **WS** 12.9"

The Say's Phoebe is found in many areas of the arid West. Like the Eastern Phoebe, they have become habituated near people and frequently nest on or around buildings. They are most often found in open habitats. As with other phoebes, these birds are solitary when not breeding. They are common to uncommon permanent residents in the Trans-Pecos and eastward to the westernmost portion of the Hill Country and northward through the western Panhandle. In the winter they can be found in small numbers well east of the breeding range, including in the western Oaks and Prairies region.

They are brown overall with a slightly darker brown head. The belly and undertail are tawny-buff. The tail is almost black and contrasts with the rump strongly.

Vermilion Flycatcher

Pyrocephalus rubinus

L 5.1–5.5" | **WS** 10"

One of the most spectacular of the flycatchers found in Texas is the male Vermilion Flycatcher—the males are quite brilliant in their bright vermilion-red plumage. There is a striking difference between the plumages of the male and female, which is unusual among flycatchers. The male has an elaborate courtship display that includes flying high above the trees and puffing out his breast as he flutters back down singing a twittering song. Vermilion Flycatchers are uncommon to common permanent residents on the South Texas Brush Country and following the Rio Grande upstream to the southern Trans-Pecos. In the breeding season they are found farther north through most to the Trans-Pecos and Hill Country. Interestingly, in the winter they move east and south to the coastal prairies.

The vermilion underparts and cap contrast with brown upperparts on the male. There is also a thin brown line that extends from the base of the bill through the eye. These birds most often perch within 15 feet of the ground.

Adult females and immature birds are grayish-brown above with a pale eyebrow.The lower belly and undertail varies from almost red to yellow.

Ash-throated Flycatcher

Myiarchus cinerascens

L 7.5–8.5" | **WS** 11.75–15.5

The members of the genus *Myiarchus* are all very similar in appearance, but location and habitat can be a big help in making an identification. Each has a distinctive voice, which is one of the best ways to tell them apart. The common member of this group in the West is the Ash-throated Flycatcher. These slender flycatchers are cavity nesters and will readily use a nest box. They are found in a variety of habitats from open woodland to mixed desert scrub. The most commonly given call is whistle-like *prrrt*. Ash-throated Flycatchers are uncommon to common summer residents in the western half of the state, east to the edge of the Rolling Plains and Hill Country. They mostly leave the state in the winter, but a few can be found along the coastal prairies as well as in the Big Bend region. Migrants and summer residents can be found from mid-March through mid-October.

They have sandy brown upperparts with rufous on the wings and tail. They have a slightly crested head and are pale yellow on the belly. In adult the tail feathers are rufous with a darker brown outer edge that expands to include the entire tip.

Great Crested Flycatcher

Myiarchus crinitus

L 8″ | **WS** 13″

The Great Crested Flycatcher is a bird of the forest. Although they are often times very easy to hear, they can be very difficult to actually see well as they prefer to stay well above the ground. Their call is a loud *wheep*. Great Crested Flycatchers are common to uncommon summer residents in the eastern half of the state as well as the eastern Panhandle. Migrants and summer residents can be found between mid-March and mid-October.

Brownish-olive upperparts with a fairly bright yellow belly. The wings have rufous edges on the flight feathers and the tail is largely rufous. Each tail feather has a darker brown edge that does not include the entire tip. The head is slightly crested.

Great Kiskadee

Pitangus sulphuratus

L 9.4″ | **WS** 16.5″

One of the more brightly colored flycatchers found in Texas is the Great Kiskadee. This is a tropical bird that reaches the northern portion of its range in the southern half of the state. These large flycatchers have a varied diet that includes insects, berries, small reptiles, and even fish. They will perch like a kingfisher low over the water and snatch small fish that are close to the surface without actually diving into the water. The distinctive coloration of the Great Kiskadee is easily recognized when seen in Texas, but there are many other tropical flycatchers that share this pattern. These chunky flycatchers are locally common in the Lower Rio Grande Valley and up the Rio Grande to Del Rio. They are uncommon up the coast to Calhoun County as well.

The head has broad black and white stripes and there is a yellow spot on the crown that is often concealed. The upperparts are brown and the underparts bright yellow. The flight feathers are bright rufous which is very obvious in flight.

Couch's Kingbird

Tyrannus couchii

L 8–9.5″ | **WS** 15.7″

The Couch's Kingbird is a bird of eastern Mexico that reaches the northern tip of its range in Texas. In Texas the vast majority of the population is migratory. They are found in the South Texas Brush Country where they can be found in areas of dense brush as well as along streams and rivers. Their distinctive *breeer* call helps distinguish them from other kingbirds. They are common to uncommon with spring migrants arriving in mid-March and most leaving the state by the end of October.

Gray upperparts with bright yellow underparts, although the chest can have a greenish appearance. The bill is rather stout and the tail is slightly forked.

Cassin's Kingbird

Tyrannus vociferans

L 8.25–9" | **WS** 16"

The yellow-bellied kingbird found in the mountains of the Trans-Pecos is the Cassin's Kingbird. They are uncommon summer residents in open woodland primarily above 4,000 feet in elevation. At the lower edge of their elevational range, they can be found in the same habitats as the similar Western Kingbird. Westerns differ in plumage and the Cassin's call is a two syllabled *chi-bew*. During migration they are common in the Trans-Pecos and uncommon to rare farther east through the western Panhandle to the western Hill Country. Migrants and summer residents can be found from April through early October.

Dark gray upperparts that include the head and chest with a strongly contrasting white chin. The belly is bright yellow and the tail is black with the hint of a pale edge on the tip.

Western Kingbird

Tyrannus verticalis

L 8–9.5″ | **WS** 14.5–15.75″

The Western Kingbirdmost is the most common and widespread yellow-bellied kingbird found in Texas. These birds can be found in almost every town and around farm and ranch houses in the western half of the state. In places where there are multiple pairs there seems to be a never-ending battle. They are common to abundant east through the Rolling Plains and Hill Country becoming more uncommon and local through the Oaks and Prairies region. Their call is a sharp *whit*. Migrants and summer residents can be found from April through early August in the eastern half of their range. Farther west migrants can be encountered through early October.

Pale gray upperparts that include the head and breast. The belly and undertail are yellow contrasting with the black tail with white outer edges.

Eastern Kingbird

Tyrannus tyrannus

L 9″ | **WS** 15″

The Eastern Kingbird is a common to locally uncommon summer resident in the eastern half of the state including the eastern Panhandle. They are most common in areas with large trees, but can also be seen in open pasturelands sitting on fences. During migration, these birds can occasionally be seen in very large flocks, particularly in the fall, when congregations can sometimes even number in the thousands of birds. Migrants and summer residents can be found from late March through early October. Eastern Kingbirds winter in South America, which makes the two well-documented records from that season in Texas remarkable.

Black above including most of the head. The underparts are white with a grayish wash across the breast. The black tail has a bold white band across the tip.

Scissor-tailed Flycatcher

Tyrannus forficatus

L 8.5–14.5" | **WS** 14.5"

The Scissor-tailed Flycatcher is an unmistakable sight in Texas. These graceful birds are common to locally abundant summer residents in all areas of the state except the western half of the Trans-Pecos. They are found in open habitats with scattered trees or shrubs where they prefer to nest. They will even use power poles if nothing more suitable is available. With its very slender body and long tail, Scissor-tailed Flycatchers are more aerodynamic than other kingbirds. Migrants and summer residents can be found from late February through early October. Small numbers can be found in winter in the South Texas Brush Country even though the majority of the population winters much farther south.

Pale gray overall with contrasting pink flanks and underwings. The tail is long and black with white outer feathers. Adult males are particularly attractive with bright pink flanks and the tail can be longer than the body. Adult females and juveniles have notably shorter tails and much paler coloration on the flanks.

Loggerhead Shrike

Lanius ludovicianus

L 8–9″ | **WS** 11–12.5″

Populations of Loggerhead Shrikes throughout North America are in decline, some very sharply. This decline is not as obvious in Texas where the areas hardest hit are primarily in the northeastern portion of the state. One of the most interesting facts about these birds is that they are accomplished predators. They have strong feet with long talon-like claws and a strongly hooked bill like a hawk, which facilitates the capture of large insects, reptiles, amphibians, birds, and small mammals. They are rare to locally common permanent residents in virtually all areas of the state. The one exception is the western half of the South Texas Brush Country where they are primarily found only in winter. They prefer open habitats.

Similar in appearance to Northern Mockingbird, but more compact. The upperparts are darker gray and they have white patches on their black wings. The underparts are white. The crown is gray contrasting with the black mask and white throat. The bill is black and sturdy with an obvious hooked tip.

Northern Shrike

Lanius excubitor

L 8.5" | **WS** 12"

Unlike the widespread Loggerhead Shrike, the Northern Shrike is a bird that is restricted in Texas to the Panhandle. As their name suggests, they are a bird of northern climes and are rare winter residents in the Panhandle, occasionally wandering south to the South Plains. They are found in Texas between mid-November and early March.

They are similar in appearance to the Loggerhead Shrike, but generally paler. In immature birds the gray tones are replaced with browns and the underparts have fine barring.

White-eyed Vireo

Vireo griseus

L 5″ | **WS** 7.5″

Vireos are generally far easier to hear than to see and the White-eyed Vireo is no different. They are found primarily in the understory of woodland and along streams where they often stay in the dense brush. Their explosive song gives away their presence as they sing almost constantly during the breeding season and with regularity at other times of the year. The song has five or six phrases and sounds as if it is singing *Get me a beer please*. They are common to uncommon migrants and summer residents in the eastern half of the state. In winter they are only found in the southern half of that region.

Olive upperparts that contrast with the gray head. Adults have white eyes that are surrounded by broad yellow spectacles, juveniles have brown eyes. They have obvious white to yellowish wing bars.

Bell's Vireo

Vireo belli

L 4.5–4.9″ | **WS** 7″

Populations of Bell's Vireo in the eastern half of the state have been in decline and they are now rare. However, these small songbirds are still locally common in the Trans-Pecos and western Hill Country. They are found in areas with fairly dense shrubs where they remain hidden most of the time. They have a complex song that consists of two phrases, the first part rising in pitch before a pause following by a similar descending phrase. Bell's Vireos are only found in the state as migrants and summer residents from late March through early October.

They are rather plain overall with olive upperparts and whitish underparts with yellow on the flanks. The head is grayish with weak, pale spectacles. The wing bars are pale and nondescript.

Black-capped Vireo

Vireo atricapilla

L 4.3 WS 7″

The Black-capped Vireo is listed as Endangered by the U.S. Fish and Wildlife Service. The southwestern Hill Country is the stronghold of this bird in the United States. Like other vireos, they are more frequently heard than seen. Their song is a raucous series of phases of two to four notes. They are a locally uncommon summer resident there and rare through the remainder of the Hill Country north to the Dallas-Fort Worth area. They are habitat specialists and require open shrublands with foliage to the ground for nesting. Heavy browsing pressure by livestock or deer can impact the quality of that habitat. Another threat to the Black-capped Vireo is nest parasitism by Brown-headed Cowbirds. For small chicks, like the vireo's, the larger cowbird chick is most often the only one that survives.

Adult males have a solid black cap that extends to just below the red eyes. They have obvious white spectacles that are broken just above the eye. The upperparts are olive-green. Females have drabber plumage with gray on the head.

Gray Vireo

Vireo vicinior

L 5.1–5.9" | **WS** 8.2"

The Gray Vireo is undoubtedly one of the most nondescript birds found in Texas, as well as one of the most infrequently encountered. Historically they were thought of as a bird of the Big Bend regions, however in the past forty years these birds seem to have expanded their range considerably to the east into the Hill Country. They are found in open shrublands and savannahs and typically defend large territories which make them harder to find as well. The song is a series of *chee cheet* phrases. They are locally uncommon to rare summer residents and are in the state between late March and early September.

Gray overall with very weak pale spectacles and wing bars that are easily overlooked. The underparts are paler.

Yellow-throated Vireo

Vireo flavifrons

L 5.5″ | **WS** 9.5″

The Yellow-throated Vireo is a true forest bird. They are consistent singers when on the breeding grounds and spend the majority of their time in the upper reaches of the canopy. They are also found in riparian woodland in the Hill Country including as far west as the Devils and Pecos River drainages. The song of the Yellow-throated Vireo is a series of phrases with long pauses between notes that sound like *thirty-eight*. Yellow-throated Vireo is a common to uncommon migrant and summer resident in the eastern half of the state. Migrants and summer residents are found between late March and September.

The head is greenish-yellow with prominent bright yellow spectacles and throat continuing down the breast to the upper belly. The remainder of the belly is white and the upperparts are gray with two bold white wing bars.

Plumbeous Vireo

Vireo plumbeus

L 4.75–5.5" | **WS** 8.7"

The Plumbeous Vireo is one of a group of vireos that was previously considered to be the same species under the name "Solitary Vireo." It is a bird of the eastern Rocky Mountains and Great Basin. In Texas, they are common summer residents in the upper elevations of the Davis and Guadalupe Mountains in oak and conifer woodland. They are also uncommon migrants through the Trans-Pecos and rare farther east from the western Panhandle south through the western Hill County. Migrants and summer residents can be found from late March through early October.

The head and upperparts are dark gray. They have bright white spectacles and the throat and underparts are white as are the two wing bars.

Blue-headed Vireo

Vireo solitarius

L 5.5″ WS 9.5″

The Blue-headed Vireo is the eastern counterpart to the Plumbeous Vireo in Texas. Although Blue-headed Vireos do not nest in Texas, they are common to uncommon migrants through the state east of the Trans-Pecos. They are also uncommon winter residents in much of the eastern two-thirds of the state south and east of the Panhandle and South Plains. Wintering individuals are most often found in flocks with other species of birds. Migrants and winter residents can be found between September and mid-May.

Olive-green above and white below with a yellow wash on the flanks. The head is gray with bold white spectacles. They also have two white wing bars.

Warbling Vireo

Vireo gilvus

L 4.5″ | **WS** 8.75″

The Warbling Vireo is a rather nondescript bird that is found throughout the United States. There are subtle differences in song and plumage between birds in the East and West that have led some to think that they may be two seperate species. In Texas both populations can be found with western birds uncommon summer residents in the Davis and Guadalupe Mountains. The nesting area for the eastern birds is from the eastern Panhandle east across northern Texas where they are also uncommon. Warbling Vireos are uncommon to common migrants in all areas of the state. Migrants are found in the spring between early April and early June and in the fall from August through mid-October.

Plain overall with gray upperparts and whitish underparts. They have an obvious whitish eyebrow and no wing bars. There can be a yellowish wash on the flanks, more prominently in fall.

Red-eyed Vireo

Vireo olivaceus

L 6″ | **WS** 10″

The Red-eyed Vireo is another vireo that is found in forests and most commonly in riparian areas. They are locally abundant to uncommon summer residents in the eastern half of the state north of the coastal prairies and South Texas Brush Country. Farther west on the Hill Country they are uncommon in riparian woodland. The muted colors of this bird makes them particularly hard to see high in the trees where they often sit in one place and sing a series *veerio-veery* phrases for long periods of time. They are common migrants through the eastern two-thirds of Texas and rare farther west. Migrants and summer residents can be found from late March until mid-October.

Olive-green above and whitish below. They have a gray crown with a black border just above a white eyebrow. The red eyes are only visible at close range in good light.

Green Jay

Cyanocorax yncas

L 11.4″ | **WS** 14.9″

When Green Jays are mentioned to birders in the United States, they automatically think of South Texas. Even though these spectacular birds can be found in many areas of Latin America, they are probably best known from Texas. They are common to uncommon permanent resident throughout the Lower Rio Grande Valley and South Texas Brush Country. The range seems to be slowly expanding northward in recent years and they have even been found in the Hill Country a few times. Despite their flashy plumage they can be very hard to spot in the dense woodland habitats they prefer.

These slender jays have a green body, brighter upperparts, and a head that is blue and black. The outer tail feathers are yellow.

Blue Jay

Cyanocitta cristata

L 11″ | **WS** 16″

The Blue Jay is a well-known bird of forests, woodland, and towns in the eastern two-thirds of the state. They are common to locally uncommon in the range, although mostly restricted to urban areas in the westernmost portion. Although these raucous birds are generally thought of as year-round residents, there is evidence of some seasonal movements within the state with large flocks seen at times. Blue Jays have wandered west well outside of their breeding range including to El Paso and this may be how populations have become established on the western edge of the range. Blue Jays cache food for later use, particularly in the fall when they will hide acorns and other items by the hundreds.

These beautifully plumaged large jays are blue above with white patches and black barring on the wings and tail. They have a crest, but it is often held flat on the crown and thus is inconspicuous.

Western Scrub-Jay

Aphelocoma californica

L 11–12″ | **WS** 15.5″

The Western Scrub-Jay is a rather slender, long-tailed jay. They are common permanent residents in the Hill Country and more uncommon and local north through the western Rolling Plains to Palo Duro Canyon. In the Trans-Pecos they are common in the Davis and Guadalupe Mountains and more local in the eastern portion to the edge of the Hill Country. The overall population appears to be declining on the eastern edge of the Hill Country as urbanization increases. They do wander some in the winter, but the only place where they are regular away from breeding areas is in El Paso. Recent research has shown that the birds from the Hill Country are genetically distinct from those in the Trans-Pecos and warrant further study.

They are grayish-blue above and grayish below with a whitish throat. Birds from the Hill Country have a much heavier bill than other Western Scrub-Jays and are not as gray on the underparts.

The birds of the Trans-Pecos are very similar with a smaller bill and slightly grayer plumage.

Mexican Jay

Aphelocoma wollweberi

L 11.4" | **WS** 13–17"

The Mexican Jay, as its name suggests, is found primarily in Mexico but they do just make it into Texas in the Chisos Mountains of Big Bend National Park. They are common permanent residents in the oak woodland of those mountains and virtually never wander away from there. Mexican Jays also can be found in the southeastern Arizona as well, although they are a different subspecies and have subtle differences, and amazingly one of those birds found its way to El Paso County. These birds have also been called "Gray-breasted Jay" in the past.

They are fairly bright blue above with a brownish cast to the back. The underparts are pale gray.

American Crow

Corvus brachyrhynchos

L 18.5″ | **WS** 36.5″

The American Crow is the large black corvid of the eastern half of Texas. They are common to abundant permanent residents east of the Hill Country and across the northern Rolling Plains to the eastern Panhandle. In the winter they irregularly wander westward into the Hill Country. American Crows are found in open habitats ranging from woodland to agricultural areas, however they have also adapted well to urban environments as well. Crows readily take advantage of roadkills and are much more adept at avoiding being hit by passing cars than are vultures. The call is a loud *CAW* that is often repeated.

Entirely black with a square tail.

Chihuahuan Raven

Corvus cryptoleucus

L 18.1–20.8" | **WS** 41–43.5"

The Chihuahuan Raven is primarily a bird of grassland and savannahs. Historically they were associated with bison herds, but they have readily adapted to modern agricultural practices. Unlike Common Ravens, these birds are migratory and can be seen in large flocks in winter and during migration. For reasons that are not readily apparent, Chihuahuan Ravens winter in very large numbers on the central Llano Estacado in the vicinity of Brownfield and Lamesa. Flocks containing more than 100 birds can be found in this area routinely during the winter. Overall they are uncommon to common year-round in most of the western half of Texas. They are generally absent from the Hill Country and the Big Bend region of the Trans-Pecos. Their voice is similar to that of the Common Raven, but is higher pitched.

Entirely black, but the bases of the feathers on the neck are white. This feature is only visible in the wind or if the bird is preening. The tail has a rounded diamond-shape.

Common Raven

Corvus corax

L 24.5″ | **WS** 46″

The Common Raven is generally seen in pairs and rarely in larger groups. These large birds are found in more rugged terrain than that of the similar Chihuahuan Raven. In Texas, they are uncommon to common permanent residents in the Hill Country and Trans-Pecos and an uncommon and local resident of the western Rolling Plains are far north as the southeastern Panhandle. The Common Ravens in Texas, and across the Southwest, are much smaller and more slender than the birds seen across Canada and in the Rocky Mountains. This makes them more difficult to separate from a Chihuahuan Raven. Their voice is a low croak.

Entirely black with longer feathers on the neck that are slightly more iridescent.

Common Ravens are known to soar high above the ground. The tail has a pointed diamond-shape.

Horned Lark

Eremophila alpestris

L 7″ | **WS** 12.5″

Horned Larks are birds of grassland that can also be found in agricultural fields and along beaches. They can be surprising common in areas that appear to be nothing more than bare ground. These are the only true larks that are found in the state. As with many other species of birds, Horned Larks are found in flocks during the winter. They are locally common to uncommon permanent residents in the Panhandle south through the northern Hill Country and along the coastal prairies. They are uncommon and local in the Trans-Pecos and eastern Rolling Plains. In winter they can be found in all areas of the state west of the Pineywoods.

Facial pattern includes a black band on the forehead that extends into small "horns" in the male and a black band that starts at the base of the bill and goes below the eye. Also a black band on the upper breast.

Purple Martin

Progne subis

L 8″ | **WS** 16″

Purple Martins are probably best known today for their use of martin houses: man-made structures for these colonial nesters. In the eastern United States these bird seem to have become dependent on these nest boxes, but in the West it is more common to find them in natural cavities. In Texas, they are uncommon to common summer residents in the eastern three-quarters of the state. As migrants, they are common to abundant and are famous for congregating in enormous roosts during the fall that can contain many thousands of birds. Purple Martins are early migrants with the first "spring" migrant reaching the state in late January. The biggest push of birds actually occurs from early March through mid-April. Fall migration takes place between early July and mid-September.

Adult males of these large swallows are entirely purplish-blue. They have a short tail that is shallowly forked and long wings.

Females and immature males are grayer overall with duller bluish-gray upperparts. The underparts are mottled white and gray and this normally extends into a collar.

Tree Swallow

Tachycineta bicolor

L 5.25" | **WS** 13"

Tree Swallows have only become a nesting bird in Texas in the past two decades. They are cavity nesters and frequently use snags in dead trees that are out in a lake. During this range expansion, they have been found on lakes from the northeastern corner of the state south through the southern Pineywoods. Tree Swallows are locally uncommon during the breeding season, but common to abundant migrants to all areas of the state. They are fairly common winter residents along the coastal prairies and more uncommon inland through the southern half of the state. Migrants and summer residents can be found from late February through November.

Adults are iridescent blue-green above and bright white below. In immature birds, the green is replaced with brown and they can have a faint breast band.

Northern Rough-winged Swallow

Stelgidopteryx serripennis

L 5″ | **WS** 11″

The Northern Rough-winged Swallow is another cavity nesting swallow. However, unlike the Tree Swallow or Purple Martin, they nest in burrows dug in dirt banks or in pipes and other man-made structures. They are common to uncommon migrants in all areas of the state as well as being rare to locally uncommon breeding birds. In the southern third of the state they can be rare to uncommon in winter as well. Spring migrants can be found between from March through mid-May and in the fall from late July through October.

Their plumage is dominated by browns with dull brown upperparts and breast. The throat is white as is the belly.

In flight they are uniform in pattern above with a square tail.

Cliff Swallow

Petrochelidon pyrrhonota

L 5″ | **WS** 11.5″

As their common name suggests, the natural nesting habitat for the Cliff Swallow is on cliffs with protective overhangs. However, they have adapted very well to human infrastructure and now are found nesting under bridges and on buildings. This has allowed their population to grow and for this species to colonize areas where nesting had not previously occurred. Cliff Swallows are common to locally abundant summer residents and are probably the most common breeding swallow in the state. Migrants and summer residents can be found between mid-February and late October.

Square tail and obvious buffy rump. The throat is dark chestnut and they have a buffy patch on the forehead.

In flight the obvious buffy rump combined with the square tail are good field marks.

Cave Swallow

Petrochelidon fulva

L 5.5″ | **WS** 11.5″

Like the closely related Cliff Swallow the Cave Swallow has adapted to nesting on man-made structures which has allowed the species to greatly expand its range. In 1960 they were only known to nest in ten limestone caves in the Hill Country, but today, they can be found over most of the state. Cave Swallows are locally common to uncommon migrants and summer residents throughout the state south of the Panhandle and west of the Pineywoods. They are also rare to locally uncommon winter residents in the southern third of the state. Migrants and summer residents can be found between February and October.

Square tail and obvious buffy rump. The throat is buffy and they have a chestnut patch on the forehead. The cap and back are dark blue and the underparts whitish.

Barn Swallow

Hirundo rustica

L 6.5″ | **WS** 12″

Like the other swallows that build mud nests, the Barn Swallow has adapted to using man-made structures for nesting areas. This tendency is now so complete, Barn Swallows arevery rarely found nesting in their traditional sites, such as caves or under rocky overhangs. They are the most widespread swallow in the world and are probably the most abundant. There is some research suggesting that males with the longest and most symmetrical tails are the ones most likely to attract a mate. Barn Swallows are uncommon to abundant migrants and uncommon nesting birds throughout the state. Migrants and summer residents can be found from mid-February through November.

Graceful flyers. In flight a white band through the tail is readily visible. Females and immature birds have shorter outer tail feathers than adult males.

Adults are blue above and buffy below with a long, deeply forked tail.

Carolina Chickadee

Poecile carolinensis

L 4 -4.75" | **WS** 6.25-8.25"

The Carolina Chickadee is the only widespread chickadee in Texas. It is very typical of the group being very active and overall gray and black in color. They are common permanent residents in the eastern half of the state including to the coastal bend and west through most of the Hill Country. In addition, the range extends westward to the eastern Panhandle and along the Canadian River. Carolina Chickadees are found in a variety of woodland and forest habitats, including along riparian corridors in the western Hill Country. They are cavity nesters and will readily use wooden nest boxes. They are very vocal, singing a high, thin *fee-bee, fee-bay* as well as the familiar *chicka-a-dee-dee-dee.*

Overall grayish, darker on the upperparts with an extensive black cap and throat with a whitish cheek. They have a tiny bill and can have a wash of pink on the flanks.

Mountain Chickadee

Poecile gambeli

L 4.75–5.5" | **WS** 8.2"

The Mountains Chickadee is a bird of the West. They are found in British Columbia south through the Rockies. The southern tip of their range is in the Davis and Guadalupe Mountains, where they are uncommon permanent residents. Here they are found in woodland habitats usually where there are at least a few pines. In the winter, they can wander down out of these habitats and have been found in the western Panhandle on rare occasions. They have similar calls to the Carolina Chickadee, but are generally more raspy or hoarse.

Overall they are grayish, darker on the upperparts. They have an extensive black cap that is split by a wide white eyebrow. The throat is also black and the rest of the head is white.

Tufted Titmouse

Baeolophus bicolor

L 6.5″ | **WS** 9.5″

The Tufted Titmouse is a common permanent resident in the woodland and forest of the eastern third of Texas, west to the western edge of the Rolling Plains and Hill Country. These birds are close relatives of chickadees but are slightly chunkier and have a noticeable crest. As with chickadees, they are cavity nesters and readily use wooded nest boxes. On the western edge of the range, Tufted Titmouse come into contact with the Black-crested Titmouse and there is narrow overlap where virtually all of the birds are hybrids. Titmice are very vocal and the most common call is a whistled *peter-peter-peter*.

They have an obvious crest most often held erect. The upperparts are gray with a black forehead and white face. The underparts are white with the exception of rusty flanks.

Black-crested Titmouse

Baeolophus atricristatus

L 6″ | **WS** 9.5″

The Black-crested Titmouse is a close relative of the Tufted Titmouse. These birds are common permanent residents through the center of the state including all of the Rolling Plains, Hill Country and South Texas Brush Country. Farther west they are found in the woodland of the larger mountains ranges with the exception of the Guadalupe Mountains where they are rare visitors. They are found in woodland and forest habitats as well as more savannah-like areas such as shrublands with scattered mottes of oaks or other larger trees. Their song is similar to that of the Tufted, but normally given at a faster pace and is harsher tones.

They have an obvious black crest that most often held erect. The upperparts are gray contrasting with the crest. The forehead is pale and the face is light gray. The underparts are white with the exception of buffy flanks.

Verdin

Auriparus flaviceps

L 3.5–4.3" | **WS** 6.6"

The Verdin is one of the smallest birds of the Southwest. One of the more interesting facets of their natural history is that they build a very large nest for their size. It is a tight ball of very small twigs held together with spider webs and has an entrance that points towards the ground. They are very active and are most often found in shrublands including those with scattered trees. Verdins are common to uncommon permanent residents in the western two-thirds of the state from the Lower Rio Grande Valley north to the southeastern Panhandle.

They are tiny with a short tail and an entirely gray body. Adults have a bright yellow face and a prominent rufous shoulder.

Bushtit

Psaltriparus minimus

L 2.75–3″ | **WS** 5.9–6.2″

Bushtits tend to stay in groups for most of the year, so it is far more common to see five or six of them than it is to encounter a single bird. These tiny birds are uncommon permanent residents through most of the Hill Country and northward through the Rolling Plains to the southeastern Panhandle. They are also found in the woodland of the higher mountains in the Trans-Pecos. Males in the populations in Mexico have a distinctive black patch on their face that is only found in immature males in the United States.

They are tiny and slender with a very long tail. Gray above and brownish below with an obvious brown cheek patch. Males have dark eyes, but in females they are pale.

Immature male with a black ear patch.

Red-breasted Nuthatch

Sitta canadensis

L 4.25" | **WS** 7.5"

Red-breasted Nuthatches, as with other nuthatches, are known for creeping head-first up, down, and along tree trunks and branches. They most often probe in the bark looking for insects, but they can also drum like a woodpecker. Red-breasted Nuthatches are irregular winter visitors to Texas. During invasion years, they can be common, particularly in the eastern half of the state, but in other years they can be virtually absent. Migrants and wintering birds are to be looked for between late September and March. During invasion years they have been found as early as late August and stayed into May.

Males generally have brighter plumage with blue-gray upperparts and reddish underparts. They have a black cap and stripe through the eye on a white face.

Females and juveniles generally have grayer stripes on the head and orangish underparts.

White-breasted Nuthatch

Sitta carolinensis

L 5.25" | **WS** 9.25"

The White-breasted Nuthatch is the largest of the nuthatches found in Texas. There are two populations in Texas that differ very subtly in plumage and voice. In northeast Texas south through the Pineywoods and in the eastern Panhandle, they are uncommon permanent residents but can be very local. Out west they are common permanent residents in the three largest mountain ranges. Elsewhere in the state, they are generally rare winter visitors except in far South Texas, where they are absent. Their presence is often given away by their frequent low-pitched *yank* calls. .

They have blue-gray upperparts with black cap and nape. The face is white which extends through the underparts with a small rusty undertail patch.

Brown-headed Nuthatch

Sitta pusilla

L 4–4.25″ | **WS** 6.25–7″

The Brown-headed Nuthatch is found only in the southeastern United States and on a couple of islands in the Bahamas. They reach the western edge of their range in Texas in the Pineywoods. They are found in pine and pine-hardwood forests throughout their range and in Texas they are locally common to rare permanent residents. They depend on large older trees to find appropriate nesting cavities since they do not use old woodpecker holes and do not make their own. These birds are much smaller than the White-breasted Nuthatch that is also found in these areas.

Small and very active with gray upperparts, a white head with a brown cap, and white underparts.

Brown Creeper

Certhia americana

L 5″ | **WS** 7.25″

The Brown Creeper is a bird that is easily overlooked. They are small and forage by creeping along the trunks and branches of trees. They will often spiral around the tree as they work their way up before flying back down to the bottom of the trunk of the same or a nearby tree. Because they basically hug the tree and are well camouflaged, it often takes a keen observer to spot them. Brown Creepers are uncommon to rare migrants and winter residents throughout the northern two-thirds of the state. These birds are generally found between late October and March.

The have mottled brown and white upperparts and white underparts. The bill is notably down curved and they have a bold white eyebrow and throat. The tail is stiff and woodpecker-like.

Rock Wren

Salpinctes obsoletus

L 4.7–5.9″ | **WS** 9″

As the name suggests, the Rock Wren is most at home on or very near the ground. They nest in rock crevices and often sing from exposed perches on rocks. They are common summer residents from the Panhandle south through the western Hill Country and Trans-Pecos. Although still present in these areas in the winter, many depart making them uncommon to rare. They are also rare and local in winter farther east into the western Oaks and Prairies region and in the South Texas Brush Country. Birds found in the winter in these areas are almost always found on dams and other areas where rocks have been placed that mimics their normal habitat.

The crown, back and wings are brown and heavily spotted with white. The rump and tail are dull rufous and contrast with the darker back. The throat and breast are pale gray with indistinct streaking and blend in with the buffy belly.

Canyon Wren

Catherpes mexicanus

L 4.3–5.9″ | **WS** 7.5″

One of the great sounds of the canyon country of western Texas is the song of the Canyon Wren. The descending series of *tew* notes is often sung from the top of a rock or from the canyon walls and can be heard echoing from a considerable distance. These fairly large wrens are uncommon to locally common permanent residents in the Trans-Pecos and Hill Country. They are uncommon and more local in the southern Rolling Plains northward to the southeastern Panhandle. They very rarely leave the canyon country, but there have been a few instances of these birds wandering east of the Hill Country.

A spectacular bird with rufous plumage heavily marked with black throughout except for a bright white throat and upper breast. The bill is long and slightly down curved.

House Wren

Troglodytes aedon

L 4.75" | **WS** 6"

House Wrens are most often found in areas with fairly dense brush where they prefer to stay hidden, but are active enough to be detected. These areas include on the edges of woodland, along riparian corridors, fence rows and shrublands in more arid areas. They are common to uncommon migrants through all areas of the state. House Wrens are uncommon to common winter resident south of the Panhandle and most common at that season on the coastal prairies and in South Texas. During the breeding season they are locally uncommon in the eastern Panhandle, particularly along the Canadian River, and in the Davis Mountains. Migrants and winter residents can be found from September through March.

They are brown overall, but darker on the upperparts. The wings and tail are barred with black and they have an indistinct pale eyebrow.

Marsh Wren

Cistothorus palustris

L 4.75" | **WS** 6.75"

Not surprisingly, Marsh Wrens are almost always found in marshes. They use dense patches of cattails or bulrush for cover and will give a sharp *tsuk* call repeatedly to alert other birds to danger. Marsh Wrens are rare to locally common winter residents throughout the state. They are locally common in summer on the immediate coast, but only east of Galveston Bay and from western Matagorda County to northern Aransas County. In the west they are rare and irregular nesters along the Rio Grande at least in Presidio County. Migrants and winter residents can be found from September through mid-May.

They have a pale face with a dark cap and a prominent white eyebrow. The upperparts are dark, but streaked with white and the underparts are grayish to buffy. The wings and tail are barred with black.

Carolina Wren

Thryothorus ludovicianus

L 5″ | **WS** 7″

In the eastern half of Texas, the Carolina Wren is the most familiar wren. They will forage around buildings and nest in flower pots that are out of the rain. The natural habitat includes open woodland where there is some brushy understory. They are common to abundant permanent residents in the eastern half of the state and uncommon in the Hill Country and Rolling Plains. They have a varied repertoire of vocalizations, but are easily recognizable by their *teakettle, teakettle, teakettle* song. Carolina Wrens are the northernmost member of a group of tropical wrens.

Rufous upperparts, including the wings and tail. They have a broad white eyebrow and are pale below with rufous on the flanks.

Bewick's Wren

Thryomanes bewickii

L 5″ | **WS** 7″

The Bewick's Wren is the most common and widespread wren in the western parts of Texas. They can be found in open woodland as well as brushy habitats and are very active and seem to have their tail cocked upward most of the time. Bewick's Wrens are uncommon to common permanent residents in the western two-thirds of the state. Formerly, these birds were present in the eastern third, but the overall populations in the eastern United States have declined dramatically in recent decades with some estimates as high as 80 percent.

Most of the birds in Texas are grayish-brown above with a contrasting gray tail. They a have a white eyebrow and are whitish below.

Cactus Wren

Campylorhynchus brunneicapillus

L 7–8.5″ | **WS** 11″

The Cactus Wren is by far the largest wren found in the United States. They are birds of open habitats and brushy places. They build a large nest, sometimes the size of a football, made of grass that is often placed in a cholla or other cactus. The male will even build more than one structure for a prospective mate to inspect and will roost in one that was not chosen for the actual nest. They are uncommon to locally common permanent residents from the Lower Rio Grande valley north to the southeastern Panhandle and west through the Trans-Pecos.

Large with a dark brown crown and heavily spotted underparts, particularly on the breast. The upperparts are grayish-brown and heavily marked with white. They have a broad white eyebrow and a decurved bill.

Blue-gray Gnatcatcher

Polioptila caerulea

L 4″ | **WS** 6.25″

The Blue-gray Gnatcatcher is a tiny, slender, and very active bird with a long tail. They are found in open woodland and forests. This species has a complex distribution in the state and are uncommon to locally common summer residents in the northern two-thirds of the eastern half of the state as well as across the Hill Country and in the Chisos and Guadalupe Mountains. In winter they are generally only found on the coastal prairies and in the South Texas Brush Country where they are uncommon, but in the last ten years they have been found farther north on numerous occasions. They are also common to abundant migrants throughout the state.

Adults are blue-gray above and white below. The tail is long and black with white outer feathers. They have a conspicuous white eye ring and white throat.

Males in full breeding plumage have a narrow black line above the eye.

Black-tailed Gnatcatcher

Polioptila melanura

L 3.8–4.25" | **WS** 5.5"

The Black-tailed Gnatcatcher is a bird of the Southwest. They are similar in structure to the Blue-gray, but very different in habitat preference. These birds are most often found in areas with at least some dense brush. This habitat is often found along desert washes where the vegetation is denser than the surround landscape. These tiny birds are the smallest songbird by weight that is found in Texas. They are common to uncommon permanent residents in the southern half of the Trans-Pecos east to the southwestern Hill Country and south along the Rio Grande in the western two-thirds of the South Texas Brush Country.

Adults are bluish-gray above and grayish-white below. The tail is long and black with thin white edges to the outer feathers. Breeding plumage males have a black cap with a white eye ring. In winter the crown in gray with a short black line over the eye.

Females lack the black cap, but are otherwise similar to the male.

Ruby-crowned Kinglet

Regulus calendula

L 4″ | **WS** 6.75″

The Ruby-crowned Kinglet is a tiny, incredibly active bird with a short tail. They never seem to stop moving as they forage through almost any terrestrial habitat from forests to urban areas to open shrublands. In the winter, they very often join in flocks with other birds as they make their way along searching for food. Ruby-crowned Kinglets are common to abundant migrants and winter residents in all areas of Texas. They are very vocal and give a *did-it* call repeatedly as they move through the landscape. Migrants and winter residents can be found from mid-September through mid-May.

Olive overall with darker wings and a short tail. There are two white wing bars and bold white crescents in front of and behind the eye.

The male has a substantial red crown patch that is usually hidden.

Eastern Bluebird

Sialia sialis

L 7" | **WS** 10–13"

The bright plumage of the male Eastern Bluebird is what most people envision when they hear bluebird. These small thrushes have declined greatly over the past two decades for reasons that are not readily apparent. In some areas in the eastern United States the installation of nest boxes along what are called "bluebird trails" seems to have had a positive effect on these birds as well as other cavity nesters. Eastern Bluebirds are uncommon to locally common summer residents in the eastern half of the state as well as the eastern Panhandle. They are also common to uncommon winter residents in all areas of the state except in the Trans-Pecos and Lower Rio Grande Valley where they are generally rare.

Males bright iridescent blue above including the wings and tail with a reddish-orange throat and breast and white belly. Bluebirds have a rather upright posture when perched.

Females are similar to males but with gray overtones to the plumage.

Western Bluebird

Sialia mexicana

L 6.5–7.5″ | **WS** 12.5″

Western Bluebirds have a much more restricted distribution in Texas than does the Eastern Bluebird. During the summer, they are uncommon and local above 6,000 feet in elevation in the Davis and Guadalupe Mountains. However, in the winter, they move into lower elevations in the Trans-Pecos as the breeding population is augmented by birds migrating into the state. Western Bluebirds can be rare to abundant in winter and can wander well to the east, although rarely east of the Hill Country. In the Trans-Pecos they are most often found in open oak-conifer woodland. Migrants and winter residents can be found from mid-September through March.

Males are deep blue above including the entire head, wings, and tail. They have a chestnut breast and grayish belly. The back has a brownish to chestnut overtone.

Females are similar to males but much grayer with some only having blue coloration on the wings, rump and tail.

Mountain Bluebird

Sialia currucoides

L 6.5–8" | **WS** 13.3"

The sky-blue color of the male Mountain Bluebird is a spectacular sight. Mountains Bluebirds are winter residents in the Trans-Pecos and in the Panhandle southward through the northwestern Hill Country. The occurrence of these birds in Texas is irruptive in nature. Some winters they can be abundant and be found in flocks containing more than fifty birds and in other years they are virtually absent. They are generally more predictable in the western third of the state, but during invasion years they can be found as far east as the western Oaks and Prairies region. They are found in open pinyon-juniper or juniper woodland. Migrants and winter residents can be found from mid-October through mid-March.

Males are sky blue with a whitish belly. The intensity of the blue varies greatly between birds.

Females are mostly gray with blue wings and on the rump and tail.

Swainson's Thrush

Catharus ustulatus

L 7" | **WS** 11.75"

The Swainson's Thrush is a member of a group of four brown, or "spotted," thrushes that are similar in appearance and behavior. Two of these, the Gray-cheeked Thrush (*Catharus minimus*) and Veery (*Catharus fuscescens*), migrate through the eastern half of the state, but are not often encountered away from woodland along the immediate coast. The Swainson's Thrush is a common to uncommon migrant through the eastern half of the state and less common farther west to the Trans-Pecos where they are rare. These thrushes are most often seen foraging on the ground and generally under shrubs where they are somewhat concealed. Migrants pass through the state during April and May in the spring and August and late October in fall.

Brownish above, sometimes with an olive overtone, and grayish below. Face buffy including the eye ring. The chest is spotted with brown which blends into the grayish belly and brownish-gray flanks

Hermit Thrush

Catharus guttatus

L 6.25″ | **WS** 12″

The Hermit Thrush is the most common small brown thrush to be found in Texas and the only one that is present in the winter. They have a habit of cocking their tail upward and then slowly lowering it as they walk on the ground foraging. Hermit Thrushes are common migrants and winter residents throughout the state. The birds that winter in the eastern half of Texas tend to be more reddish brown on their upperparts than those in the west. This is because they are from two different breeding regions, but there is considerable mixing and eastern and western birds can be found together through the central part of the state. Migrants and winter residents can be found from late September and mid-May.

Similar to Swainson's Thrush but with an obviously bright rufous tail. The face is browner and the eye ring much narrower. They are gray-brown above with a white throat and breast with brown spotting.

Wood Thrush

Hylocichla mustelina

L 7.75″ | **WS** 13″

The Wood Thrush is the largest and chunkiest of the small brown thrushes. Their liquid song consisting of multi-note phrases is a favorite sound at dawn in the forests of East Texas. Wood Thrushes are uncommon to locally common summer residents in the forests of east Texas and are locally uncommon in the Lost Pines region near Bastrop. They are common to uncommon migrants through the eastern half of the state, but are more common in spring than in fall. As with many other trans-Gulf migrant songbirds, Wood Thrushes are often easier to see in the woodland habitats found along the immediate coast during migration.

Bright rufous upperparts and white underparts that are boldly spotted with black. The crown is bright rufous as well and the face is white dense dark streaking.

Clay-colored Thrush

Turdus grayi

L 9″ | **WS** 17″

The Clay-colored Thrush is a tropical species that has expanded its range northward steadily in recent decades. Prior to the 1990s, they were rare visitors to the Lower Rio Grande Valley with the first nesting record discovered in 2002. Now they are uncommon to rare permanent residents. They inhabit native thorn scrub woodland as well as urban habitats. In the last ten years, they have been found in areas farther north and are now resident up the Rio Grande to the Laredo area and they are of increasing regular occurrence up to coast to Corpus Christi.

Brownish-olive above and tawny below. Unlike an American Robin they lack white markings around the eye. The throat is paler than the rest of the head and has light brown streaking. The bill is dull yellow.

American Robin

Turdus migratorius

L 9.5″ | **WS** 14″

The American Robin is one of the most familiar birds in all of North America to the point that it is often considered the harbinger of spring or winter even though they are year-round residents in almost all of the United States. In Texas, they are common to locally abundant winter residents in the northern two-thirds of the state and uncommon farther south. In the summer they are uncommon in the northern half of the state east of the Pecos River and locally in El Paso and the Guadalupe Mountains. They seem to be expanding their breeding range southward in the eastern half, especially in urban areas.

Brown above with a notably darker head and orange on the underparts. They have prominent white marking around the eye and the throat is white with black streaking. In adult males the head is black and the underparts bright orange. Females are very similar to males, but with duller plumage.

Gray Catbird

Dumetella carolinensis

L 8.5″ | **WS** 11″

Gray Catbirds are rather secretive birds and spend most of their time in areas of dense vegetation. Like some other thrashers, they are able to mimic other sounds and the call is only vaguely similar to a cat. Gray Catbirds are uncommon to common migrant through the eastern half of the state and uncommon to rare farther west. In winter, they are locally uncommon to rare along the coastal prairies and Lower Rio Grande Valley but there have been instances of bird wintering well inland. Gray Catbirds are also uncommon to rare breeders across northern Texas and south through the Pineywoods.

Dark gray overall with a black crown and rusty undertail.

Curve-billed Thrasher

Toxostoma curvirostre

L 10.6" | **WS** 13.3"

The Curve-billed Thrasher is a bird of the Southwest, and other than Northern Mockingbird, the most familiar thrasher in that region of the country. They have an elaborate song, but the loud even toned *whet-whet* call is given frequently. Curve-billed Thrashers are uncommon to locally common permanent residents in the western half of the state east to the eastern edge of the Rolling Plains and Hill Country. They are found in open brushy habitats ranging from mixed desert scrub to oak and mesquite savannahs and even urban habitats.

Uniformly gray-brown overall with lighter underparts with indistinct spotting on the breast. Long tailed with broad white tips and they have an obviously orange eye.

Brown Thrasher

Toxostoma rufum

L 11.5″ | **WS** 13″

Brown Thrashers spend a lot of time foraging on the ground, although not exclusively. These rather brightly colored thrashers have an elaborate song where each phrase is repeated two times. They are similar in pattern to the "spotted" thrushes, but the long bill and notably long tail are keys in separating them. Brown Thrashers are uncommon to locally common summer residents from the eastern Panhandle eastward across the northern Rolling Plains and through the Pineywoods. They are also a common migrant and winter resident across the eastern half of the state becoming increasing less common farther west. They use a wide variety of brushy habitats including woodland with an understory. Migrants and winter resident occur between mid-September and April.

They have fairly bright rufous upperparts including the long tail and the wings have two white wing bars. The throat and underparts are white with dark rufous and black streaking.

Long-billed Thrasher

Toxostoma longirostre

L 10.2–11.4" | **WS** 13"

The Long-billed Thrasher is very similar in appearance to the Brown Thrasher and has similar habits. They are found in brushy habitats ranging from open arid scrub to dense vegetation along riparian corridors. They are common to uncommon permanent residents from the southern edge of the Hill Country southward through the South Texas Brush Country. Long-billed Thrashers are a specialty of South Texas, but unlike many of the birds in this category they have only a small range in eastern Mexico. The song is very similar to their close relative, the Brown Thrasher, with phrases repeated two or three times. The call is a load whistled *cheeooep*.

The upperparts are grayish-brown as is the long tail and the wings have two white wing bars. They have a gray face and a white throat and underparts that are streaked with black. The bill is long and slightly down curved.

Northern Mockingbird

Mimus polyglottos

L 10″ | **WS** 14″

The Northern Mockingbird is an abundant to common permanent resident throughout the state and is the state bird of Texas. There are few other birds that are as conspicuous, abundant, and widespread as the Northern Mockingbird. They are found in a variety of semi-wooded habitats including urban areas, grassland with scattered woody vegetation, and open woodland. About the only places they are not found are in closed-canopy forests. They are best known for their incredible ability to mimic the songs of other birds as well as other sounds. They most often sing from exposed perches high above the ground and will sing both day and night during the height of the breeding season.

They are gray above and white below. The wings are darker with two white wing bars and a conspicuous white patch. The tail is long with wide white borders.

European Starling

Sturnus vulgaris

L 8.5″ | **WS** 14″

The European Starling is native to Europe and Asia and has become widely introduced elsewhere in the world. The first birds released in North America were at New York City in the 1890s. These birds thrived and the population started expanding westward. Amazingly the first bird found in Texas was only thirty-five years later. They are now found throughout the lower forty-eight states, southern Canada and northern Mexico. They are abundant to common permanent residents throughout most of the state, but they are most common in urban habitats and around human habitations. In many rural areas, they are rare to uncommon at best.

They are short-tailed and pudgy with short legs. Adults in summer plumage are iridescent bluish-purplish overall with a yellow bill.

In the winter they are iridescent green and have white-tipped feathers on the underparts. The bill is dark with a pale base.

Juvenile birds are ashy gray overall and normally seen in the company of adult birds.

American Pipit

Anthus rubescens

L 6″ | **WS** 10.5″

American Pipits are sparrow-like in appearance but have a thin bill. They spend virtually all of their time walking around the edges of wetlands, fields, and grassland foraging for insects. It is quite common to encounter them in small flocks, but very large concentrations are possible. American Pipits are common to uncommon migrants and winter residents throughout the state. They can be found in the state between late September and April. The very late lingering birds will begin molting in the bright buffy underparts of breeding plumage before they migrate. They give a sharp *pip-pit* call in flight.

They are uniformly brown above with two whitish wing bars and longish tail with white edges. The face has a pale eyebrow and throat. The underparts are whitish with dark streaking on the breast and flanks.

Cedar Waxwing

Bombycilla cedrorum

L 6″ | **WS** 10.25″

The spectacular Cedar Waxwing is something of a nomad during the winter. They are notoriously unpredictable in where they can be found in any given winter and their presence is generally associated with fruiting trees and shrubs. They feed on berries most commonly, but will also eat fresh buds. They get their name from the odd waxy red tips on their flight feathers. Cedar Waxwings can be common to abundant migrants and winter residents in all areas of the state. The timing of their arrival varies greatly from year to year, but in general they can be found between September and April. Migrants are occasionally encountered as late as early June and these birds are presumed to be individuals that wandered far south.

Elegant with brown upperparts and a gray rump. The tail has a bold yellow band across the tip. They have a brown crest and head with a black mask. The breast is also brown fading into the yellow belly.

Phainopepla

Phainopepla nitens

L 7–8.2" | **WS** 11.4"

The Phainopepla is one of the most elegant birds in Texas. These slender birds are part of a small tropical family known as silky-flycatchers. They feed on insects and fruit, but are particularly fond of mistletoe berries. One study showed that a single Phainopepla can consume up to 1,000 mistletoe berries in a single day, when available. The common name is also the genus name and is Greek for "shinning robe." They are rare to locally uncommon permanent residents in the Trans-Pecos, but do wander eastward some in the fall.

The males are silky black overall with an obvious crest and a red eye. The inner webbing of the primaries is white and obvious when seen in flight. Females are a uniform brownish-gray with an obvious crest.

Ovenbird

Seiurus aurocapilla

L 4–6″ | **WS** 9.5″

The Ovenbird is part of a fairly large family of insectivorous birds known as warblers. Ovenbirds are most likely to be encountered as they walk—not hop—on the ground and forage in the leaf litter. They prefer forest or woodland habitats that have a well-developed understory, but in migration they can be found in any shrubby habitat. They are common to uncommon migrants through the eastern half of the state and uncommon and local in winter in the Lower Rio Grande Valley and immediate Gulf Coast. Migrants may be found from late March through mid-May and between late August and early October.

Superficially resembling a thrush, these warblers typically walk along the ground often with their tail slightly raised. They have olive upperparts and white underparts with bold black streaking. The crown is orange broad black stripes on either side.

Northern Waterthrush

Parkesia noveboracensis

L 5–6″ | **WS** 9.5″

Both species of waterthrushes occur in Texas, though only Louisiana Waterthrush (*M. motacilla*) breeds here. They are ground-dwelling warblers with brown plumage and are streaked below. They are most commonly found walking along the edge of water from wetlands to rivers and streams. The Northern Waterthrush is the most widespread of the two, but the Louisiana Waterthrush is equally common in the east. Northern Waterthrushes are common to uncommon migrants in the eastern half of the state and uncommon to rare through the western half. Migrants may be found during April and May and between mid-August and mid-October.

Uniformly brown upperparts with a whitish or buffy eyebrow. The throat is white or buffy and heavily streaked as are the underparts. While foraging this waterthrush constantly bobs its tail.

Black-and-white Warbler

Mniotilta varia

L 5.25" | **WS** 8.25

The Black-and-white Warbler has a different foraging technique than other warblers and is more like a nuthatch. They creep along the trunk and branches of a tree looking for insects. Black-and-white Warblers are one of a very few warblers that are present in Texas throughout the year. A migrant throughout the state, they are uncommon to common through the eastern three-quarters and generally rare in the Trans-Pecos. These warblers are uncommon nesting birds in the eastern third and west through the Hill Country and an uncommon winter resident in the southern third of Texas. Migrants and summer residents can be found between late March and late October.

The adult male has a striking black-and-white striped plumage. Adult females and juveniles are much whiter, particularly on the face and underparts.

Tennessee Warbler

Oreothlypis peregrina

L 4.75″ | **WS** 7.75″

The Tennessee Warbler is strictly a migrant through Texas. They are uncommon to common through the eastern half of the state in the spring. They can be abundant at woodland habitats along the coast as well as in the Pineywoods during this time. However, in the fall they are uncommon to rare. These birds are trans-Gulf migrants, meaning they fly across the Gulf of Mexico rather than around it, and as a result they are decidedly less common in the western half of the state. Spring migrants can be found from late March through mid-May and from late August to late October in the fall.

Adult males in breeding plumage are bright green above with a gray crown and nape. They have a white eyebrow and a dark line through the eye on an otherwise white face. They are white below including the undertail.

Adult females in the spring are drab olive-gray above and pale yellow below. The undertail coverts are white in all plumages. In the fall males are similar in overall coloration.

Orange-crowned Warbler

Oreothlypis celata

L 5″ | **WS** 7.5″

The Orange-crowned Warbler is one of the most common migrant warblers in Texas. Rather drab in overall coloration and the lack of flashy field marks is a clue in identifying them. Orange-crowned Warblers from various breeding areas in North America make their way to Texas in the fall and these birds vary considerably in the amount of yellow that is in their plumage. Migrants pass through the state between late March through mid-May in the spring and primarily in October in the fall. Orange-crowned Warblers reported in late August and September are more likely immature Yellow Warblers.

Non-descript with grayish upperparts with some wash of yellowish color. The face can be pale yellow including an eyebrow and the pale yellow extends in to the underparts, especially on undertail.

Some individuals can be much more yellow overall, but share the same basic plumage pattern.

Colima Warbler

Oreothlypis crissalis

L 5.1″ | **WS** 7.8″

In the United States, the Colima Warbler is restricted to the upper elevations of the Chisos Mountains in Big Bend National Park. They are an uncommon and extremely localized summer resident in the oaks and maples of the more mesic canyons. They were initially discovered on the wintering grounds in the state of Colima, Mexico in 1889, thus the common name. Although they are the most common nesting warbler in the Chisos Mountains, being familiar with their trilling song helps to locate them. These birds arrive in late April and are usually present until early September.

Gray head with reddish cap and white eye ring. The gray continues through the underparts and the upperparts and flacks are brownish. The rump and undertail are golden-yellow.

Nest in depressions on the ground, usually under a root mass or rock overhang.

Nashville Warbler

Oreothlypis ruficapilla

L 4.25″ | **WS** 7.25″

The Nashville Warbler is another of the more common migrants warblers found in Texas. They are uncommon to abundant migrants through almost all of the state. They are mostly circum-Gulf migrants, so they do not fly out over the Gulf and as such they are much less common close to the coast from Galveston eastward especially in the spring. Migrants pass through the state between late March through late May in the spring and primarily from mid-August through October in the fall.

Bright adult males have a gray hood with a white eye ring and a small rufous cap that is often concealed.

Adult females and many birds encountered in the fall are much drabber in overall plumage.

MacGillivray's Warbler

Geothlypis tolmiei

L 3.9–5.9″ | **WS** 7.5″

The MacGillivray's Warbler is the western half of a pair of sister species. The eastern bird is the Mourning Warbler (*G. philadelphia*), which lacks the bold white eye crescents of the MacGillivray's and has a more prominent black chest patch. These birds prefer dense understory, even during migration. MacGillivray's Warblers are uncommon to rare migrants through the western half of Texas. Spring migrants can be found from early April through early June and from late August to early October in the fall.

Males have a well-defined slaty gray hood with black lores and bold white eye crescents. There is a small black patch on the chest. The upperparts are olive-green and the underparts yellow.

Females have a notably paler gray hood which makes the eye crescents less obvious.

Kentucky Warbler

Geothlypis formosa

L 5.25″ | **WS** 8.5″

The Kentucky Warbler is another ground-loving warbler. Like most of the other warblers that share this trait, these warblers are found in woodland with a well-developed understory, which allows them to forage in the leaf litter and find protection. They are uncommon to locally common migrants through the eastern third of the state. In addition, they are rare to locally uncommon nesting birds from northeast Texas south through the Pineywoods and west to the Lost Pines region around Bastrop. Migrants and summer residents can be found between late March and late September.

The upperparts are entirely olive contrasting with the bright yellow underparts. Adult males have a black crown, mask, and sideburn with a yellow eyebrow and throat.

Adult females and juveniles are very similar with paler markings on head.

Common Yellowthroat

Geothlypis trichas

L 4.75″ | **WS** 6.75″

The Common Yellowthroat is a common warbler in cattail marshes or other wetlands where tall emergent vegetation is abundant. They often remain hidden and can be very difficult to detect. Fortunately they have a strong *chuck* call and a memorable *witchety-witchety-witchety-witch* song. Common Yellowthroats are permanent residents across the northern Panhandle, in the eastern quarter of the state, on the coastal prairies, and along the Rio Grande, including tributaries such as the Devils and Pecos Rivers. They are common migrants to all areas of Texas and a common to uncommon winter resident south of the Panhandle. Migrants and winter residents are found from early September through May.

Adult males have a prominent black mask bordered on top by broad whitish line. Birds in the East have an olive or brownish band across the belly.

Adult females and juveniles are less dramatically plumaged with grayish-olive upperparts and yellowish and olive underparts.

Hooded Warbler

Setophaga citrina

L 5.25″ | **WS** 7″

The Hooded Warbler is one of the first warblers to return to the nesting ground each spring. They are found in woodland and forests with an understory. They spend most of their time close to the ground and actually nest on the ground. Hooded Warblers are common to locally abundant summer residents in the eastern quarter of the state and locally west to the Lost Pines region. They are also an uncommon to common migrant through the eastern third of the state are generally rare farther west. Migrants pass through the state between mid-March and mid-May and from mid-August through October.

The adult male is unmistakable with the sharply defined black hood surrounding a yellow face. With olive upperparts and yellow underparts this active warbler is often observed on or near the ground fanning its tail, exposing the brilliant white on the inner webbing of the outer feathers.

Adult females and juveniles have an olive crown and upperparts. Some females have some black on the forehead and a discontinuous bib.

American Redstart

Setophaga ruticilla

L 5.25″ | **WS** 7.75″

The American Redstart is a fascinating bird to watch as it continuously fans its tail and flicks it wings as it forages. They are uncommon to locally common migrants in the eastern half of Texas becoming uncommon to rare in the west. They are also rare to locally uncommon nesting birds in the forested areas of East Texas. Spring migrants can be found from early April through mid-May and from mid-August to October in the fall.

The adult male is distinctive with largely black plumage highlighted by patches of orange on the sides of the breast and in the wings and tail. They have a white belly.

Adult females are greenish-olive above with yellow patches in the wings and tail. The head is gray with weak white spectacles and throat; the underparts are whitish with yellow patches on the sides of the breast.

Northern Parula

Setophaga americana

L 4.5″ | **WS** 7″

The Northern Parula is another warbler that nests in Texas. Found in open woodland and forest, these tiny warblers show a preference for nesting in clumps of Spanish moss (*Tillandia usneoides*). They are not limited by the presence of this epiphytic plant, but it can be an important part of the habitat. Northern Parulas are common to uncommon migrants through the eastern half of the state. They are also uncommon to common summer residents in the eastern half of the state including west to the eastern Rolling Plains and farther west across the Hill Country. Migrants and summer residents can be found between late February and October.

Adult males are blue-gray above with a greenish back and have two white wing bars. They have white marking around the eye with a yellow throat and underparts. A blue-gray breast band may be present as this trait varies in intensity depending on the individual.

Adult female and immature birds have a similar pattern to the males but paler and lack the breast band.

Tropical Parula

Setophaga pitiayumi

L 4.3″ | **WS** 6.2″

The Tropical Parula is the southern counterpart of the Northern Parula. They have a very large distribution through Latin America but are restricted to Texas in the United States. Tropical Parulas are mostly found in open oak woodland in Texas and there are two nesting areas that are surprisingly far apart. The largest population is in the eastern portion of the South Texas Brush Country between Kingsville and Raymondville. In the last two decades they have also colonized the woodland found along the Devils and Pecos Rivers. Overall they are rare to locally uncommon summer residents in both areas and rare during that season in the Lower Rio Grande Valley. Summer residents can be found from late March to mid-September.

Blue-gray above with a greenish back and has two white wing bars. They have black lores and an orange breast band and are, in general, similar in coloration to the Northern Parula.

Magnolia Warbler

Setophaga magnolia

L 5″ | **WS** 7.5″

The Magnolia Warbler is one of the more strikingly plumaged warblers to pass through Texas. These birds molt on the breeding grounds prior to making the fall migration and the males at that season have a plumage pattern very similar to the females. They are uncommon to common migrants through the eastern half of the state. As is the case with many neotropical migrants, Magnolia Warblers are often found in larger numbers and more frequently in wooded habitats along the coast. Spring migrants can be found from mid-April through May and from September through October in the fall.

Spring males spectacular with bright yellow underparts heavily streaked with black. The tail pattern is unique among the warblers and is black with a wide white band.

Adult females and winter plumaged males are similar with often indistinct streaking on underparts and a gray head.

Bay-breasted Warbler

Setophaga castanea

L 5.5″ | **WS** 9″

Bay-breasted Warblers have an odd migration path in that they are uncommon to common migrants through the eastern third of Texas in spring, but rare to very rare in the fall, when they are primarily found father east. Like the Magnolia Warbler, the Bay-breasted Warbler molts on the breeding grounds and the fall plumage is much plainer than in the spring. The overall population has declined in recent decades and this change has been readily evident in the number of birds found during spring migration. Spring migrants can be found from mid-April through May and from September through October in the fall.

Spring males have chestnut on the crown, breast, and flanks. The back is gray with black streaking and the wings have two white wing bars. The face is black with a buffy patch on the neck.

Adult females are generally gray with a hint of a chestnut cap and with varying amounts of chestnut on the sides of the breast. Winter plumaged males are similar with a yellowish cast on the underparts.

Chestnut-sided Warbler

Setophaga pensylvanica

L 5″ | **WS** 7.75″

The Chestnut-sided Warbler is another of the distinctively marked warblers that migrates through the state. As with some others, these warblers molt on the breeding grounds and look very different between the spring and fall. Chestnut-sided warblers are uncommon to locally common spring migrants and uncommon to rare in the fall. Spring migrants can be found from mid-April through May and from early August through mid-October in the fall.

Spring males are largely white with a yellow crown and black eyelines and whiskers that form a T on the face. The underparts are white with a chestnut stripe on the flanks. Adult females are similar but with duller plumage.

In the fall they have green crowns and upperparts with a pale face. Males have some chestnut on the flanks, but many females and immature birds do not.

Yellow Warbler

Setophaga petechia

L 5″ | **WS** 7″

The Yellow Warbler is another of the very common migrants through Texas. This warbler breeds throughout much of the United States and Canada, but the only nesting population in Texas is the very distinctive Mangrove Warbler. This subspecies is found in mangroves and coastal scrub on the southern tip of South Padre Island, as well as in similar habitats in northern Latin America. The Yellow Warbler is a common to abundant migrant through all areas of the state and the Mangrove Warbler is a permanent resident. Spring migrants can be found from late March through May and from late July through mid-October in the fall.

Adult males are bright yellow overall with an unmarked head. The underparts are streaked with red and the tail has paler yellow spots on the webbing of the outer feathers.

Adult females and juveniles are drab yellow with unmarked breast.

Male Mangrove Warbler has entirely chestnut head.

Pine Warbler

Setophaga pinus

L 5.5″ | **WS** 8.75″

The Pine Warbler is a fairly large warbler and, as its name suggests, is found in pine forests. In Texas that puts them in the pine forests in the eastern quarter of the state and locally farther west to the Lost Pines region in the vicinity of Bastrop. They are permanent residents in these areas, but in the winter they are uncommon throughout the eastern half as migrants from northern populations reach the state. Farther west they are generally rare, but in some winters larger numbers make their way onto the Hill Country in particular. Migrants and winter residents occur from early October through late March.

Adult males are largely yellow with an unstreaked back and white wing bars. They have olive-yellow upperparts, including the crown with contrasting yellow around the eye and throat.

Females and immature birds are much drabber yellow and can even be largely gray.

Yellow-throated Warbler

Setophaga dominica

L 5.5″ | **WS** 8″

The Yellow-throated Warbler is found in the pine forests of the eastern quarter of Texas, but also occurs in cypress-sycamore communities along rivers across the southern Oak and Prairies region and westward across the Hill Country all the way to the Devils River. They are fairly large warblers and are more deliberate in their actions when foraging than many other warblers. They are uncommon to locally common as a summer resident and as a migrant through the eastern half of the state. They are also rare to locally uncommon winter residents along the coastal prairies and in the Lower Rio Grande Valley. Spring migrants can be found from late February through early May and from late July through late September in the fall.

Upperparts gray with two white wing bars. Black on cheek continues down as streaks on the side of the breast bordering bright yellow throat. Prominent white eyebrow and underparts.

Yellow-rumped Warbler

Setophaga coronata

L 5″ | **WS** 8.25″

The Yellow-rumped Warbler is a common to abundant migrant and winter resident throughout Texas. The eastern and western populations were once considered separate species and both occur commonly in the state. The western population is known as the "Audubon's" Warbler and they are the predominate birds found in the western half of Texas. They are also uncommon and local nesters in the Davis and Guadalupe Mountains. The "Myrtle" Warbler is the eastern population and they are abundant in the eastern half of the state and fairly common in the west. These two populations may be considered as separate species again. Migrants and winter residents occur from early September through mid-May.

The adult male "Myrtle" Warbler is gray above streaked with black with a black mask and white throat. The underparts are white with a heavily streak breast with yellow patches on the sides. They have a conspicuous yellow patch on the rump. Females are similar, but drabber.

The adult male "Audubon's" Warbler is darker overall with yellow throat and large white patches on the wings.

Many of the wintering birds in Texas are immature and are very drab, but the white or yellow throat is normally easy to determine.

Grace's Warbler

Setophaga graciae

L 4.75″ | **WS** 8″

The Grace's Warbler is the western counterpart of the Yellow-throated Warbler and is similar in appearance. They are uncommon summer residents in pine woodland in the Davis and Guadalupe Mountains. The population in the Davis Mountains has been greatly impacted by fires and drought that have killed a very high percentage of the Ponderosa (*Pinus ponderosa*) and southwestern white pines (*Pinus flexilis*). They are rarely seen during migration even though they are known to pass through the western half of the Trans-Pecos. The summer residents are found from mid-April through mid-September.

Gray above with some black marking on the crown and back and a bright yellow eyebrow and throat; the remainder of the underparts are white streaked with black on the flanks.

Townsend's Warbler

Setophaga townsendi

L 4.75″ | **WS** 8″

The Townsend's Warbler is one of the more common migrants through the mountains in the Trans-Pecos. They are uncommon to common as they pass through the higher elevations and uncommon to rare at lower elevations and eastward through the western High Plains and Hill Country. They are rare to very rare in winter along riparian areas at low elevations in the Trans-Pecos and in the Lower Rio Grande Valley. Spring migrants can be found from early April through late May and from early August through early November in the fall.

Adult males have an intricate black and yellow pattern on the head. The upperparts are olive streaked with black with two white wing bars.

Adult females and juveniles are similar to the adult male but generally lack the black throat and the pattern on the face is dark olive.

Golden-cheeked Warbler

Setophaga chrysoparia

L 4.7–5.1″ | **WS** 8″

The breeding range of the Golden-cheeked Warbler is entirely within the state of Texas. They are found only in oak-juniper woodland on the Hill Country and northward to the vicinity of Possum Kingdom Lake. They are dependent on strips of bark from mature Ashe juniper (*Juniperus ashei*) to construct nests.They are uncommon at rare summer residents and rarely detected as migrants. They can be locally common such as at Lost Maples State Natural Area. Spring migrants start arriving in very early March and most have departed by early August.

Adult males have a bright yellow cheek with a black eyeline that separates the yellow into two parts. The upperparts and crown are black with two obvious white wing bars.

Adult females have a paler yellow cheek and lack the black throat. Their upperparts are olive streaked with black.

Black-throated Green Warbler

Setophaga virens

L 5.25″ | **WS** 7.75″

The Black-throated Green Warbler is closely related to the Golden-cheeked Warbler. They are so similar that a singing migrant can elicit a territorial response from a Golden-cheeked. Black-throated Green Warblers are common to uncommon migrants through the eastern half of the state. They are more regular farther west than many of the eastern warblers and are uncommon in the eastern Hill Country. They are also locally uncommon to rare winter residents from about Corpus Christi south on the Coastal Prairies to the Lower Rio Grande Valley. Spring migrants can be found from mid-March through late May and from early August through mid-November in the fall.

Adult males have a yellow cheek patch and olive upperparts. They have a black throat and upper breast; the underparts are otherwise white with a small yellow patch near the undertail.

Adult females and juveniles have a white throat with some varying amounts of black. The black on the underparts is greatly reduced, particularly in immature females.

Wilson's Warbler

Cardellina pusilla

L 4.25″ | **WS** 6″

Wilson's Warbler is another of the widespread migrant warblers in Texas. They are uncommon to common migrants throughout the state, but are most common in the western third of Texas where they can be abundant. The population that breeds from Alaska south through the Rocky Mountains are brighter in color, particularly on the face, than those from the eastern subspecies. Wilson's Warblers are also uncommon to rare winter residents in the Lower Rio Grande Valley and northward through the southern Coastal Prairies. Spring migrants can be found from late March through late May and from early August through October in the fall.

The adult male has an obvious black cap. The upperparts are olive-yellow and the underparts bright yellow. The female lacks the black cap.

Green-tailed Towhee

Pipilo chlorurus

L 7" | **WS** 9.8"

The Green-tailed Towhee nests through the southern Rocky Mountains and westward across the Great Basin. The two small breeding populations in the Davis and Guadalupe Mountains are isolated from the main range of this species. Green-tailed Towhees are common to uncommon migrants and winter residents through the western half of the state. Brushy areas make up the preferred habitat during the winter. Migrants and winter residents are present from early September through mid-May.

The upperparts, wings, and tail are grayish-olive. The dull rufous crown and gray face contrast strongly with the white throat.

Spotted Towhee

Pipilo maculatus

L 6.75–8.25″ | **WS** 10.5″

The Spotted Towhee was formerly considered part of the same species as the Eastern Towhee (*P. erythrophthalmus*) under the name "Rufous-sided Towhee." The Spotted is the more common of these two sister species and is a common to uncommon migrant and winter resident throughout the western two-thirds of the state. In the upper elevations of the Guadalupe, Davis, and Chisos Mountains, they are uncommon to locally abundant in the summer. As with other towhees, the Spotted Towhee frequently forages on the ground where they kick back and forth with both feet through leaf litter. Migrants and winter residents are found from late September through late April.

The upperparts are mostly black with heavy white spotting on the wings and back. The long tail has white corners. Prominent rusty flanks and a white belly are present on both males and females though males are typically the darker of the two.

Canyon Towhee

Melozone fuscus

L 8.2–9.8″ | **WS** 11.8″

The Canyon Towhee is a large ground-loving sparrow of the Southwest. These curious birds seem to adapt well to human development and will enter buildings looking for food. They are uncommon to common permanent residents through the Trans-Pecos and Hill Country and northward through the western Rolling Plains to the canyonlands in the southeastern Panhandle. Open areas with scattered shrubs are their preferred habitat, but areas of denser brush are also used. The remarkable duet call of *squeechurrrrrr!* can be heard echoing through the canyons in the summer.

This towhee is long in shape and light brown overall, including the wings and tail. The crown is pale rufous over gray cheeks and a buffy throat. There is an obvious dark spot on the breast.

Olive Sparrow

Arremonops rufivirgatus

L 5.3–5.9″ | **WS** 8.6″

The Olive Sparrow is a bird that tends to stay in dense brush where they spend a considerable amount of time foraging on the ground. The vast majority of their range is in Mexico and northern Central America, but they are common permanent residents in the South Texas Brush Country. The southern edge of the Hill Country marks the northern boundary of the range where they are uncommon west to the Devils River. As with many other species, these birds seem to be slowly expanding northward.

The upperparts, including the wings and tail are olive; the underparts are gray with olive on the flanks. The head is gray with rufous-brown stripes on the crown.

Rufous-crowned Sparrow

Aimophila ruficeps

L 5.1–5.9″ | **WS** 8.3″

The Rufous-crowned Sparrow is a large sparrow preferring rocky slopes and other open habitats. Nesting takes place on the ground as does the majority of foraging. They are common to uncommon permanent residents through the Trans-Pecos and Hill Country and northward through the western Rolling Plains to the eastern Panhandle.

Overall grayish with rufous streaking on the back. The crown is dull rufous over a gray face with a prominent white eye ring and a blackish whisker mark.

Cassin's Sparrow

Peucaea cassinii

L 5.1–5.9″ | **WS** 8″

The Cassin's Sparrow is a bird of open grassland, although they will tolerate some encroachment by woody vegetation. The breeding display involves the male flying up well above the ground and fluttering back down while singing. The song is a loud trill followed by two notes and is one of the great songs of grassland birds. Cassin's Sparrow is a common to abundant summer resident through the western half of the state and an uncommon to rare permanent resident in the Trans-Pecos and Hill Country southward. Summer residents are found from mid-March through early September.

A rather drab sparrow with a long tail, large bill and flattened crown. The crown, nape and upperparts are heavily streaked with rufous-brown and the underparts are uniformly brown.

Bachman's Sparrow

Peucaea aestivalis

L 4.8–5.9″ | **WS** 7.8″

The Bachman's Sparrow is an endemic bird of the great pine forests of the southeastern United States. Management of these forests to produce a pine savannah with limited undergrowth is important for these birds. They are rare to locally uncommon permanent residents in the Pineywoods. Populations in eastern Oklahoma and western Arkansas supposedly winter in Texas, but there does not seem to be a notable increase in abundance in the winter.

A long-tailed sparrow with primarily brown plumage. The upperparts are heavily marked brown and rufous. The face and breast are buffy blending into the whitish belly.

American Tree Sparrow

Spizelloides arborea

L 5.5″ | **WS** 9.5″

Over the past half century, the southern extent of the wintering range of the American Tree Sparrow has steadily moved northward. In the 1950s these birds were rare, but regular, winter birds in the northern Hill Country. Today they are only found in the Panhandle and most commonly in the northern half of their region. They are most often found in brushy habitats, particularly along drainages and in canyons in the eastern Panhandle. Winter residents are found from November through mid-March.

The face and underparts are uniformly gray. The crown is dull rufous as is line behind the eye. The back is brown and heavily mottled with black and white and there are two white wing bars. The base of the lower mandible is yellow.

Chipping Sparrow

Spizella passerina

L 5.25″ | **WS** 8.25″

The Chipping Sparrow is one of the most common wintering sparrows in Texas. They are often found in large groups as well as in mixed flocks with other species. These small, slender birds are found in a variety of habitats from open woodland to grassland with scattered shrubs. They frequently forage on the ground and have a habitat of squatting down in the grass making them easy to overlook until they flush. Chipping Sparrows are common to abundant migrants and winter residents throughout the state south of the Panhandle where they are generally rare. They are also common summer residents in the Davis and Guadalupe Mountains of the Trans-Pecos, the Hill Country and the Pineywoods. Migrants and winter residents are found between mid-August and mid-May.

A small slender sparrow with upperparts mottled black and brown, two white wing bars and underparts that are light gray. A black line runs through the eye on the gray face. The crown shows a thinly streaked rusty cap.

In the height of breeding plumage the crown is bright rufous and the markings on the face more conspicuous with a black bill.

Clay-colored Sparrow

Spizella pallida

L 4.9–5.5″ | **WS** 7.8″

The Clay-colored Sparrow nests across Canada and the northern most part of the United States, but despite this wide nesting range, they funnel down the Great Plains during migration. This makes them a common to uncommon migrant from the eastern Trans-Pecos to the edge of the Pineywoods. They are often encountered in fairly large flocks and they readily mix with flocks of Chipping Sparrows. They primarily winter in Mexico, but small numbers are also found at that season in the western South Texas Brush Country and irregularly farther north into the western Hill Country and Trans-Pecos. Migrants are found between early September and early November in the fall and from mid-March through mid-May in the spring.

This small sparrow has upperparts mottled with black and brown and is grayish underneath. The face is well marked with a well-defined brown ear patch surrounded by gray. The crown is heavily streaked with brown.

Field Sparrow

Spizella pusilla

L 5.75" | **WS** 8"

The Field Sparrow has an oddly disjunct breeding range in the state with somewhat isolated breeding populations in various areas. They are uncommon in the northern Pineywoods, Hill Country, eastern Panhandle, and eastern South Texas Brush Country. In the Rolling Plains they are oddly rare and local and typically occur in isolated areas between better established populations. Field Sparrows are common to uncommon migrants and winter residents in all areas of the state except the Trans-Pecos where they are rare. The preferred habitat is open shrublands and savannahs. Migrants and winter residents can be found between mid-September and early May.

A small slender sparrow with an entirely pink bill; the head is grayish with a rufous cap, nape and stripe behind the eye. The upperparts are mottled with rufous and black and the underparts range from buffy to gray.

Black-chinned Sparrow

Spizella atrogularis

L 4.9–5.9″ | **WS** 7.8″

Although closely related to the Chipping, Clay-colored, and Field Sparrows, the Black-chinned Sparrow is very different in appearance and much more regional in distribution. In fact these birds are more likely to be confused with a Dark-eyed Junco than a Chipping Sparrow. Black-chinned Sparrows are uncommon summer residents in the mountains of the Trans-Pecos. There is an altitudinal migration and they are uncommon and more localized in the winter, suggesting that some part of the population moves farther south. Open habitats with abundant grasses, including savannah-like woodland, are the preferred habitat in the summer and brushy areas are used in the winter as well.

A small slender sparrow with a gray head and underparts; the upperparts are brown and heavily mottled with black. Males in breeding plumage have a black chin that extends up and around the base of the pink bill. Females have smaller area of black on the face if any.

In winter the sexes are similar with no black on the face.

Vesper Sparrow

Pooecetes gramineus

L 5.75″ | **WS** 9.5″

The Vesper Sparrow along with the Savannah Sparrow are the most common grassland sparrows that winter in the state. Vesper Sparrows are uncommon to common migrants and winter residents in most of the state. In the winter, they are generally absent from the Panhandle. Although they do not nest any closer than north-central New Mexico, there are a few summer records from the Panhandle and South Plains. Migrants and winter residents can be found between mid-September and early May.

This medium sized sparrow is brown overall with the face and upperparts heavily mottled with brown. A rufous shoulder patch is sometimes present but can be hidden. The long tail shows white outer tail feathers which can be a helpful clue to the bird's identity.

Lark Sparrow

Chondestes grammacus

L 6–6.75″ | **WS** 11″

The Lark Sparrow is one of the more boldly marked sparrows with a distinctive head pattern. Savannah-like habitats are preferred but they seem to prefer to perch closer to the ground on fences or the tops of shrubs. Lark Sparrows have an exceptionally musical song which led to the common name of lark. They are common to uncommon migrants and summer residents throughout most of the state. They retreat from the northern two-thirds in winter and are rare to locally uncommon on the Coastal Prairies and South Texas Brush Country. Migrants and summer residents are found from late March through early October.

The head displays a prominent white stripe down the center of the crown bordered by chestnut stripes. The face is boldly marked with a bright chestnut ear patch bordered by white. The white throat contrasts strongly with a bold black whisker stripe. The upperparts are brown with black streaking and the underparts are gray with brownish flanks and a black spot on the center of the breast.

Black-throated Sparrow

Amphispiza bilineata

L 4.75–5.5″ | **WS** 8.6″

The Black-throated Sparrow is often thought of as a bird of the low desert and is usually the most common bird in that habitat however they are much more widespread. They are common to abundant permanent residents through the Trans-Pecos and east through the Hill Country and southern Rolling Plains as well as most of the South Texas Brush Country. They can be found from very open desert scrub to open savannah to shrublands. Black-throated Sparrows spend a lot of time on the ground and will join roving feeding flocks in the winter.

This sparrow has a stunning face pattern with two broad white stripes and a black throat that extends down the breast. The upperparts are brownish-gray with paler underparts. The tail is darker than the back with small white tips of the outer feathers.

Lark Bunting

Calamospiza melanocorys

L 5.5–7″ | **WS** 11″

The breeding range of the Lark Bunting is basically the Great Plains extending from southern Saskatchewan south to the northern Panhandle of Texas. They are locally uncommon summer residents there becoming rare and irregular south to the northwestern Hill Country. Lark Buntings are abundant to uncommon migrants and winter residents through the western half of the state. Fall migrants start to arrive as early as mid-July and can be common during August. Spring migrants are present from May with a few lingering into June. Grassland and open shrubland are the preferred habitat for these sparrows.

Winter plumaged birds are brown overall with fairly uniform upperparts and paler underparts heavily streaked with brown.

Breeding plumaged males are black with a conspicuous white wing patch.

Savannah Sparrow

Passerculus sandwichensis

L 5″ | **WS** 8.25″

Savannah Sparrows are the most abundant wintering grassland sparrow in Texas. Despite the fact that grassland is the preferred habitat, these small sparrows can be found in savannahs, open shrublands, weedy areas, agricultural areas, and even along the edges of denser woodland. They are uncommon to abundant migrants and winter residents throughout the state. Migrants and winter residents are present from mid-September through early May.

A heavily streaked sparrow overall with brown upperparts marked with black; the underparts are white with the breast streaked with brown and a breast spot. The head is strongly patterned with a dark crown and pale eyebrow with yellow lores of varying intensity.

Song Sparrow

Melospiza melodia

L 5.75″ | **WS** 8.25″

Although not restricted to wetland habitats, the Song Sparrow certainly favors those areas. Other habitat types are used, especially during migration, including open woodland, hedgerows, grassland with scattered woody vegetation, and weedy fields. They are common to uncommon migrants and winter residents across the state north of the South Texas Brush Country where they are rare. Migrants start to arrive in late September and most have left the state by late April.

Heavily streaked overall with brown upperparts marked with black. The underparts are grayish with brown streaking and a breast spot. The head is gray with a dark crown split with a pale stripe through the middle, a rufous stripe behind the eye and a black whisker.

Lincoln's Sparrow

Melospiza lincolnii

L 5.5" | **WS** 7.75"

The Lincoln's Sparrow is another of the confusing heavily streaked sparrows. They are common to uncommon migrants through all areas of the state. In the winter, they are common to locally abundant in the southern two-thirds of the state and uncommon to rare farther north. This sparrow is typically found in brushy habitats ranging from open woodland to grassland with patches of woody vegetation. Migrants and winter residents are found between late August and mid-May.

Grayish-brown overall and heavily streaked above and below, the steep forehead gives the bird a slightly crested look when alert. The head is gray with a dark crown split with a pale stripe through the middle, a dark stripe behind the eye and a broad buffy whisker.

The streaking on the underparts restricted to the breast and flanks. A buffy colored breast contrasts with the slightly chestnut color of the wings.

White-throated Sparrow

Zonotrichia albicollis

L 6–7″ | **WS** 9″

The White-throated Sparrow is part of a group of fairly large sparrows that have boldly patterned crowns. They are found in weedy fields, along hedgerows, and other brushy habitats including in open woodland. An uncommon to locally common migrant and winter resident in the eastern half of the state they become increasing less common and more localized in the west. Warm days will trigger bouts of singing throughout the winter, which increases as spring arrives. The song is a clear whistled *Sam Peabody, Peabody, Peabody*. Migrants and winter residents can be found between the last few days of October through late April.

A large sparrow with boldly striped black and white crown (in some individuals the white is replaced by tan) and bright yellow lores. The throat is a bright white surrounded by gray. The upperparts are brown mottled with black and the underparts are gray.

Harris's Sparrow

Zonotrichia querula

L 6.5–8″ | **WS** 10.5″

The Harris's Sparrow is a large sparrow of hedgerows and weedy places. They nest in northern Canada and migrate down through the center of the continent to the wintering grounds on the southern Great Plains. In Texas, this includes from the eastern High Plains across to the eastern edge of the Oaks and Prairies region and southward through the eastern Hill Country to the northern edge of the Coastal Prairies. They are uncommon to locally common within this range between very late October and mid-April.

In the winter this sparrow has a tan head and a pinkish bill. The crown is heavily mottled with black and the face has varying amounts on black depending on age and sex.

Prior to migration in the spring, this sparrow molts into breeding plumage which is similar to winter plumage but with a full black face and crown that contrasts strongly with the gray face.

Dark-eyed Junco

Junco hyemalis

L 6″ | **WS** 8.5″

The Dark-eyed Junco was once considered to be a complex of four species. All are easily identifiable and three are present in the winter in Texas. These birds are very often encountered in large flocks and in the western half of the state can include all three identifiable forms. Juncos are uncommon to abundant migrants and winter residents in the northern two-thirds of the state. They use a wide variety of habitats ranging from open woodland to dense brush. Migrants and winter residents can be found between early October and mid-April.

The "Slate-colored" Junco of the East is gray overall with a bright white belly. The tail is long with white outer feathers.

The "Oregon" Junco is a group of similar looking subspecies with blackish or gray hoods and pinkish sides. This is a "Pink-sided" Junco.

The "Gray-headed" Junco is a bird of the Rocky Mountains and is gray overall with a red back.

White-crowned Sparrow

Zonotrichia leucophrys

L 6″ | **WS** 9.5″

The White-crowned Sparrow is by far the most common of the large ornately plumaged sparrows. They are abundant to uncommon migrants and winter residents. Weedy and brushy habitats are preferred, but they also can be found in urban areas and even in grassland with some woody vegetation. Migrants and winter residents are present from mid-September through May. Three subspecies occur in Texas, birds that nest in the northern Rocky Mountains have white lores and those from the southern Rockies and from Canada have black lores.

Adults have a gray head with bold black and white crown stripes. These lores can be white (as here) or black.

Immature birds have a brown and tan striped head.

Summer Tanager

Piranga rubra

L 6.75" | **WS** 12.2"

Of the four species of tanagers that occur in Texas, the Summer Tanager is the most common and widespread. Although these birds retain the name tanager, they are not actually even closely related to the true tanagers of the neotropics. They are instead closely related to grosbeaks and buntings. The Summer Tanager is a rare to locally common summer resident throughout the eastern half of the state and westward across the Hill Country and Trans-Pecos. They are also uncommon to common migrants through all areas of the state. Migrants and summer residents can be found from early April through October.

Adult males are entirely red with a thick yellowish bill. They retain the red plumage throughout the year.

Adult females and juveniles wholly dull yellow overall, although some individuals can be orange-yellow.

Western Tanager

Piranga ludoviciana

L 6.5–7.75" | **WS** 11.4"

The Western Tanager is the widespread tanager of western North America. They are uncommon to locally common summer residents in the Davis and Guadalupe Mountains. These mountains as well as some others southern Arizona are the southernmost breeding areas. Western Tanagers are uncommon to common migrants through the western third of the state, although individuals are regularly found much farther to the east. Adult males molt in August and lose the bright breeding colors. Migrants can be found between Mid-April and late May and from late August through early October.

Adult males in breeding plumage are bright yellow with a black back, wings and tail. The shoulder is yellow with a single white wing bar. The head is red, varying in intensity, with a pale bill.

Adult females and juveniles are yellow with a gray back and yellow rump. The wings are darker with a yellow upper and white lower wing bar.

Northern Cardinal

Cardinalis cardinalis

L 8.75″ | **WS** 12″

The Northern Cardinal is a very familiar bird throughout most of Texas. They are common to abundant permanent residents east of the Pecos River and uncommon to locally common in the southern Trans-Pecos and generally absent from the northern half of the region. There is evidence of some seasonal movement within the state, but this is difficult to detect because of their general abundance. Both male and female Northern Cardinals will sing at almost any time of the year. The song is a series of whistles that resembles *purty purty purty* and accelerating toward the end.

Adult males are bright red overall with a black face and prominent crest. The bill is large and reddish.

Adult females are brownish overall with a red on the face, crest and wings.

Pyrrhuloxia

Cardinalis sinuatus

L 8.2″ | **WS** 11.8″

The Pyrrhuloxia, a close relative of the Northern Cardinal, is typically found in arid habitats in the Southwest. They sound very similar and share the prominent crest and heavy bill. Both species also occur in the same areas throughout most of the Pyrrhuloxia's range in Texas. The Pyrrhuloxia is a common to uncommon permanent resident in the Trans-Pecos and eastward through the western Hill Country and south through the South Texas Brush Country. Unlike most birds, they move northward in the winter where they are uncommon on the South Plains and eastward through much of the Rolling Plains and eastern Hill Country.

Adult males are gray overall with red on the face and down through the middle of the underparts. They also have red on the prominent crest as well as the wings and tail. The bill is more rounded than a Northern Cardinal and yellow. Adult females are grayish with red on the crest, wings, and tail.

Rose-breasted Grosbeak

Pheucticus ludovicianus

L 8″ | **WS** 12.5″

The Rose-breasted Grosbeak is rather stocky and very deliberate in its movements, which make it appear lethargic at times. These birds are found in woodland and forest habitats as they pass through the state and are particularly attracted to mulberries in the spring. Rose-breasted Grosbeaks are common to uncommon migrants through the eastern half of the state becoming increasing less common farther west. Migrants can be found between early April and late May and from mid-September through early November.

The black and white plumage of the adult male is striking. A large red patch on the breast contrasts strongly with the white underparts. The black wings have two white wing bars.

Adult females and juveniles are brown and tan above. The head is largely dark with a wide white eyebrow and stripe below the ear patch. The underparts are whitish-buff with brown streaking.

Black-headed Grosbeak

Pheucticus melanocephalus

L 7–7.4″ | **WS** 12.5″

The male Black-headed Grosbeak is one of the more brightly colored birds of the mountains of the Trans-Pecos. These birds are common summer residents in the higher elevations of the main mountain ranges and an uncommon migrant through the western half of the state. Black-headed Grosbeaks nest above 5,000 feet in elevation in oak-juniper woodland. Despite their western range, these birds regularly wander eastward and are rare in winter along the coastal prairies. Migrants can be found between early April and late May and from mid-September through late October.

A stocky bird with an orange belly and collar; the back, wings and tail are black. The rump is also orange and they have two white wing bars.

Adult females have a gray head with a wide white eyebrow and stripe below the ear patch. The underparts have a buffy-orange wash of varying intensity. Immature males look very similar with brighter underparts.

Blue Grosbeak

Passerina caerulea

L 5.9–6.2″ | **WS** 11″

The Blue Grosbeak is found in open spaces ranging from savannahs to grassland with at least a few scattered shrubs. It is not uncommon to see these birds sitting on roadside fences or feeding on the ground. They are locally common to uncommon summer residents throughout most of the state, only avoiding forest habitats. Migrants and summer residents can be found from early April through mid-October.

Adult males are a vibrant dark blue with rufous wing bars. They are fairly large birds with a gray conical bill. They remain blue throughout the year.

Adult females are brown overall with tan wing bars. The large bill helps distinguish them from the small buntings.

Indigo Bunting

Passerina cyanea

L 5.5" | **WS** 8"

The diminutive male Indigo Bunting is one of the very few birds found in Texas that is entirely blue. These birds are common to abundant summer residents through the eastern half of the state and more uncommon and local west through the Rolling Plains and Hill Country. The nesting habitat is most often secondary growth in old fields and pastures and along riparian corridors. Indigo Buntings are also abundant migrants through the eastern half of the state and uncommon through the remainder of the state east of the Pecos River. They are also locally uncommon in winter in the Lower Rio Grande Valley. Migrants and summer residents can be found from late March through Mid-October.

Adult males are vivid blue in breeding season and the head is often slightly darker that the body. In the fall they are brown with some blue on the rump and in the tail.

Adult females and juveniles are uniformly drab brown though the brown is somewhat paler on the underparts. Faint streaking is often present on the breast and buffy wing bars are noticeable.

Varied Bunting

Passerina versicolor

L 4.3–5.5″ | **WS** 8.2″

When seen in good light, the unique purple plumage of the male Varied Bunting makes it one of the most spectacular birds in Texas. They are locally uncommon to rare summer residents in the southern Trans-Pecos and eastwards across the southern half of the western Hill Country. In the western South Texas Brush Country, including the western Lower Rio Grande Valley, they are rare and local at that season. Varied Bunting favor shrubby habitat in canyonlands for breeding and can be found in riparian woodland as well. Migrants and summer residents can be found from mid-April through mid-September.

The adult male is stunning year-round with purple body plumage and a light blue forehead and red crown. The rump is also pale blue.

Adult females and juveniles are very plain brown overall. Some individuals will have some blue on the rump and tail.

Painted Bunting

Passerina ciris

L 4.7–5.1″ | **WS** 8.6″

Despite the spectacular colors of the male Painted Bunting, they are more often heard than seen. They often sing from a concealed perch and the rapid series of musical chips is often the best way to detect them. In brushy habitats in the southern Rolling Plains and Edwards Plateau they are often one of the most common breeding birds. Painted Buntings are uncommon to common summer residents and migrants throughout most of the state. The only areas where they do not nest are the open country of the High Plains and in the northern Trans-Pecos. Migrants and summer residents can be found from mid-April through mid-September, although most adult males have left the state by mid-August.

Adult male is unmistakable with green upperparts, a blue head, and red body. Plumage retained year-round.

Adult females and juveniles drab greenish overall often with lighter upperparts.

Dickcissel

Spiza americana

L 5.5–6.2" | **WS** 9.8"

Dickcissel are well-known to stop their migration when they encounter favorable nesting conditions in a particular area. In dry years, they continue migrating, so the overall population varies tremendously from year to year. They are uncommon to abundant migrants through the eastern three-quarters of the state and uncommon to rare in the Trans-Pecos. They nest in weedy areas, grassland, and pastures. The song is usually written as "*dick, dick, dick, sissel-sissel*". Migrants and summer residents can be found from early April through late October.

Rather large-headed with a wide conical bill. The short tail gives the bird a compact appearance. The upperparts are mottled brown and black and the wing has a distinct rusty shoulder. Adult males are unmistakable with a gray and yellow head and a black bib on a bright yellow breast.

Adult females are similar in overall pattern but much drabber.

Red-winged Blackbird

Agelaius phoeniceus

L 8″ | **WS** 14″

The Red-winged Blackbird is one of the most common and widespread birds in North America. They can be abundant in the marsh habitats where they nest, but that is nothing compared to the incredibly large congregations that can be found in the winter. They are abundant to locally uncommon migrants and summer residents in the eastern half of the state and more localized in the west where nesting habitat is more restricted. In winter the resident population is bolstered by migrants from farther north.

Adult males are entirely black except for the large red shoulder patch that is bordered by yellow on the trailing edge.

Adult females and juveniles are brown and heavily streaked overall. Their size and long pointed bill help separate them from similarly plumaged sparrows.

Eastern Meadowlark

Sturnella magna

L 9.5″ | **WS** 14″

Meadowlarks are true grassland and savannah birds. The Eastern Meadowlark is a locally common to rare summer resident in the eastern half of the state ranging west through the Rolling Plains to the eastern Panhandle. A separate population that may even be a separate species is an uncommon resident in the grassland of the Trans-Pecos. They are locally common to rare in migration and winter throughout the remainder of the state. The eastern population has declined dramatically in the past forty years and has all but disappeared from some areas.

A very chunky bird with a short tail, they are mottled brown and tan above with a prominently striped head. In breeding plumage the lores and throat are bright yellow, as are the underparts, with a large black V on the breast. In winter they are much duller and the yellow much more subdued.

Brewer's Blackbird

Euphagus cyanocephalus

L 8–10″ | **WS** 14.5″

The Brewer's Blackbird is a common to locally abundant migrant and winter resident throughout out the state, although generally more common in the western half. These birds are almost always encountered in flocks and can be present in very large concentrations especially in agricultural areas and around livestock feed lots. Brewer's Blackbirds are also well adapted to urban habitats as well. Migrants and winter residents can be found between mid-September and mid-May.

Adult males have a yellow eye and are entirely black with blue and purplish iridescence. They can be confused with the Common Grackle, which has much a longer, keel-shaped tail and longer bill.

Adult females have brown eyes and are grayish-brown overall with notably darker wings and tail.

Common Grackle

Quiscalus quiscula

L 12.5″ | **WS** 17″

Grackles are characterized by their large size and long, keel-shaped tails. In Texas, the Common and Great-tailed Grackles are found throughout much of the state, while the Boat-tailed (*Quiscalus major*) is restricted to the coast. The Common Grackle is a common to uncommon summer resident from the Panhandle southeastward through the Rolling Plains and eastern Hill Country to the central coast. They are common to abundant in winter in the eastern half of the state and uncommon to rare west across the South Plains and Hill Country and in the northern two-thirds of the South Texas Brush Country. Migrants and winter residents can be found from mid-September through late May.

Adults are entirely black with purplish iridescence on the head. The body has a bronzy iridescence with a long, keel-shaped tail and pale eyes.

Great-tailed Grackle

Quiscalus mexicanus

L 15–18″ | **WS** 22.8″

The Great-tailed Grackle has undergone an amazing northward range expansion during modern times. In 1900 they were restricted to the South Texas Brush Country. Now, however, they are abundant residents in all areas of the state except the forests of East Texas where they are restricted to urban areas. This expansion extends north to Nebraska and west to California. They have become a particular nuisance during the winter months, especially at lighted parking lots with scattered trees. Thousands will descend on these areas to roost leaving massive amounts of droppings and causing other damage.

Adult males are very large with a keel-shaped tail. They are entirely black with purplish-blue iridescence and a yellow eye.

Females are tawny-brown with darker wings and tail.

Brown-headed Cowbird

Molothrus ater

L 8″ | **WS** 11–14″

The Brown-headed Cowbird is probably best known for laying their eggs in the nests of other species. The eggs of these birds have been found in an astounding 220 host species and of those 144 are known to have successfully raised a cowbird. Brown-headed Cowbirds are common to locally abundant summer residents throughout the state. In the winter, the majority of these birds withdraw from the Trans-Pecos, Hill Country and Pineywoods, although they are still locally common during that season. The overall wintering population increases with migrants from farther north and enormous winter roosts can form, especially in urban areas.

Adult males have a brown head and black body with a dark eye.

Adult females are brownish-gray overall, but somewhat darker on upperparts.

Orchard Oriole

Icterus spurius

L 7.25″ | **WS** 9.5″

Orioles are a group of more brightly colored blackbirds. The smallest of this group found in Texas is the Orchard Oriole. They are uncommon to locally common summer residents in the eastern two-thirds of the state, but excluding the South Texas Brush Country. They are also locally uncommon breeders in the Trans-Pecos. They are uncommon to common migrant throughout most of the state, but are rare in the El Paso area. Migrants and summer residents can be found from very late March through early October.

A small, slender oriole with a slightly decurved bill; adult males are black above with a chestnut rump and shoulder patch. The head and upper breast are black and the remainder of the underparts chestnut.

Adult females are yellow with a gray back and two white wing bars. Immature males are similar but with a black face and bib.

Hooded Oriole

Icterus cucullatus

L 7–8″ | **WS** 10.6″

The Hooded Oriole is a slender orange oriole found in the southern parts of the state. They are uncommon and local summer residents in the South Texas Brush Country northward through the southwestern Hill Country and west along the Rio Grande to the Big Bend area. In Brooks and Kenedy counties, they are most common in the oak woodland. The Hooded Orioles found in Texas are brighter orange than those found farther west in Arizona and California. Summer residents arrive in as early as late March and are present until early October.

Adult males are primarily orange with a black face and bib, back, wings and tail. They have two white wing bars and the bill is thin and slightly decurved.

Adult females are yellowish-orange with a gray back and have two slender white wing bars.

Bullock's Oriole

Icterus bullockii

L 6.6–7.5″ | **WS** 12.2″

The Bullock's Oriole is a common to uncommon summer resident in the western half of the state. They were once considered part of the same species as Baltimore Oriole under the name "Northern Oriole." Recent studies have shown that they are distinct and in fact are not each other's closest relative. As migrants Bullock's Orioles are common to uncommon east to the eastern edge of the Rolling Plains and Hill Country. Migrants and summer residents can be found between late March and late September.

Adult males are primarily orange with a black crown, nape, and back. There is a black line through the eye and a black throat. The wings are black with a large white patch.

Adult females have dull orange on the head and undertail with a gray belly and upperparts. The wings are gray with white wing bars.

Altamira Oriole

Icterus gularis

L 8.25–10″ | **WS** 14.1″

The Altamira Oriole is a specialty of the Lower Rio Grande Valley. These large orioles were first discovered in Texas in 1938 and were rather rare in the United States until the early 1960s when the population began to grow. Now they are uncommon residents of the native thorn-scrub habitat along the Rio Grande through Zapata County. Some observers now believe that the population is starting to decline.

A large orange oriole with a black face and bib; the back, wings, and tail are black with an orange shoulder and one white wing bar that extends into a patch as the base of the flight feathers.

Baltimore Oriole

Icterus galbula

L 7″ | **WS** 11.5″

The Baltimore Oriole is the common orange-plumaged oriole of the East and the only one likely to be encountered east of the Rolling Plains and Hill Country. They are common to uncommon migrants through the eastern half of the state and can be locally abundant along the Coastal Prairies. Baltimore Orioles are also locally uncommon summer residents in the eastern Panhandle and east across northernmost counties along the Red River. Migrants are found from early April through May and from late July through late October. They were once considered the same species as the western Bullock's Oriole.

Adult males are orange with a black head, back, and wings. They have an orange shoulder and one white wing bar.

Adult females are mottled gray above with gray wings and two white wing bars. The head and breast are yellow-orange.

Scott's Oriole

Icterus parisorum

L 9″ | **WS** 12.5″

The Scott's Oriole is most often associated with the arid habitats of the Southwest. They are in fact common to uncommon summer residents across the Trans-Pecos and eastward through the Hill Country to Travis and Bexar counties. They can be found from open desert habitats to open oak-juniper woodland. These yellow orioles are present from mid-March through early October.

Adult males have a black head and breast with bright yellow underparts. The back and wings are black with a bright yellow shoulder and one white wing bar.

Adult females are yellow with a strong gray wash over the head. The upperparts are gray with two white wing bars.

House Finch

Haemorhous mexicanus

L 5.25″ | **WS** 8.75″

The House Finch has an interesting history. They are native to western North America, but were introduced into New York City in 1940. This population expanded rapidly and reached the eastern edge of Texas in the early 1990s. These birds have now reached the native populations of the West. House Finches are uncommon to locally common permanent residents in all areas of the state except the southern South Texas Brush Country where they are still rare.

Adult males have a broad red to pinkish-red eyebrow, throat, and breast. The upperparts are brown with the exception of the reddish rump. The underparts are pale but heavily streaked with brown.

Adult females are brown overall with paler underparts heavily streaked with brown.

Pine Siskin

Spinus pinus

L 5″ | **WS** 9″

Pine Siskins are somewhat nomadic during the winter, searching for food and taking up residence when they find it. These heavily streaked finches can be common to abundant during some winters and difficult to find in other years because of this behavior. They can be found in all areas of the state and are readily attracted to feeders, particularly those with thistle seed. The timing of occurrence in a given year varies greatly but in general they can be found between early October and mid-May. Interestingly, lingering birds have remained and nested a few times in the Panhandle and Trans-Pecos.

This siskin is brown overall and very strongly streaked with a thin, pointed bill. The upperparts are brown with black streaking and the wings and tail have yellow patches. The amount and brightness of yellow varies depending on age and sex.

Lesser Goldfinch

Spinus psaltria

L 5″ | **WS** 7.8″

The Lesser Goldfinch is an uncommon to locally abundant migrant and summer resident in the Trans-Pecos, Hill Country, and South Texas Brush Country. They are also uncommon to rare northward through the Rolling Plains to the southeastern Panhandle and seem to be increasing in numbers in this region. Most of the birds in the Rolling Plains and Hill Country withdraw in the winter. Migrants and summer residents can be found from mid-March through mid-November.

Adult males in Texas are solid black above and bright yellow below. They have white markings in the wings including a large patch at the base of the primaries.

First-year males have a black cap and wings that contrast with a green back. Adult males in California and Arizona retain this plumage into adulthood.

Adult females and juveniles are greenish-yellow with white wing markings.

American Goldfinch

Spinus tristis

L 4.5–5″ | **WS** 7.5–8.75″

The American Goldfinch is an uncommon to abundant migrant and winter resident throughout the state. As with the Pine Siskin, the number of birds present in a given winter varies greatly depending on food availability. By the time these birds reach Texas in the fall, the bright yellow plumage of the male has been lost and only a few remain in the state long enough in the spring to molt back into that bright plumage. Migrants and winter residents can be found from early September to late April with a few lingering as late as early June.

Winter plumaged birds have a yellow face with brown upperparts and white underparts. Adult males, like this one, have very black wings with white wing bars. Females and immature birds have grayer wings and the wing bars can be buffy.

The breeding plumaged male is bright yellow with a black cap, wings, and tail. They have white wing bars and the undertail is pale.

House Sparrow

Passer domesticus

L 6.25" | **WS** 9.5"

The House Sparrow is a European bird that was introduced to North America. The first releases were in Brooklyn, New York in the 1850s and they quickly spread. They were also released in Galveston in 1867 and quickly became established. House Sparrows are now uncommon to locally abundant, primarily in urban areas and around human habitations, throughout the state. There is some evidence that populations in Texas are beginning to decline.

A big-headed bird with a short tail. Adult males have a broad chestnut band behind the eye that extends to the back which is heavily marked with black. The crown and cheek are gray with a black chin and upper breast.

Adult females and juveniles are drab brown above and gray below with a broad pale eyebrow.

Author Acknowledgements

I started birding in Texas roughly 40 years ago. I have been fortunate enough to travel to all regions of the state and to bird with many very skilled observers during that time which allowed me to start building an understanding of the status and distribution of the avifauna of the state. This foundation has allowed me to participate in the activities of the Texas Bird Records Committee since 1995 and to be the regional editor for the Texas column in North American Birds since 1994. I would particularly like to thank Greg Lasley, Brush Freeman, and Willie Sekula for our many interactions that helped to shape my understanding of our birds. I thank Brush Freeman and Doug Booher for their many thoughtful comments on previous drafts of this book.

—Mark Lockwood,
Alpine, Texas

Scott & Nix Acknowledgments

Many thanks to Mark Lockwood, and to Jeffrey A. Gordon, Louis Morrell, and everyone at the American Birding Association for their good work. Special thanks to Curt and Joe Matthews at Independent Book Publishers (IPG) along with his colleagues, Mark Voigt, Mark Noble, Jeff Palicki, Michael Riley, Mary Knowles, Cynthia Murphy, and many others. Thanks to Alan Poole, Miyoko Chu, and especially Kevin J. McGowan at the Cornell Lab of Ornithology. We give special thanks to Brian E. Small for his extraordinary photography and to all the others whose images illuminate this guide, including Bob Steele, Alan Murphy, Jim Zipp, and the photographers represented by VIREO (Visual Resources for Ornithology). We thank Rick Wright for his excellent work on the manuscript; editorial interns Vicki Scott, Harry Kidd, and Paul Pianin were invaluable; James Montalbano of Terminal Design for his typefaces; and René Nedelkoff and Nancy Heinonen of Four Colour Print Group for shepherding this book through print production.

Image Credits

(T) = Top, (B) = Bottom, (L) = Left, (R) = Right, (M) = Middle, (TL) = Top left, (TR) = Top right, (BL) = Bottom left, (BR) = Bottom right; pages with multiple images from one source are indicated by a single credit.

XIII–8 Brian E. Small. **9** Brian E. Small (T)(BL), Mark W. Lockwood (BR). **10–34** Brian E. Small. **35** Alan Murphy. **36–45** Brian E. Small. **46** Brian E. Small (T), Mark W. Lockwood (B). **47–55** Brian E. Small. **56** Brian E. Small (L), Mark W. Lockwood (R). **57** Brian E. Small (L), David Salem (R). **58** Brian E. Small. **59** Alan Murphy (L), Brian E. Small (R). **60** Brian E. Small (L), Alan Murphy (R). **61** Brian E. Small. **62** Alan Murphy (L). **62** Brian E. Small (R). **63** Brian E. Small (L), Alan Murphy (R). **64** Brian E. Small (T), B.K. Wheeler/VIREO (B). **65** Brian E. Small. **66** Alan Murphy. **67** Brian E. Small (T), G. Lasley/VIREO (B). **68–78** Brian E. Small. **79** Brian E. Small (T), Alan Murphy (B). **80–96** Brian E. Small. **97** Brian E. Small (T), R. Curtis/VIREO (B). **98–99** Brian E. Small. **100** Mark W. Lockwood. **101** Brian E. Small. **102** Brian E. Small (T), Alan Murphy (B). **103–104** Brian E. Small. **105** Brian E. Small (T), Alan Murphy (B). **106–108** Brian E. Small. **109** Mark W. Lockwood. **110–114** Brian E. Small. **115** M. Hyett/VIREO. **116–120** Brian E. Small. **121** Brian E. Small (T), Alan Murphy (B). **122–123** Brian E. Small. **124** Mark W. Lockwood. **125–126** Brian E. Small. **127** Mark W. Lockwood. **128–130** Brian E. Small. **131** Brian E. Small (T), J. Turner MD/VIREO (B). **132–134** Brian E. Small. **135** Alan Murphy (T), Brian E. Small (B). **136** Brian E. Small (L), Alan Murphy (R). **137–145** Brian E. Small. **146** Brian E. Small (T), Alan Murphy (B). **147** David Salem. **148–164** Brian E. Small. **165** G. Bartley/VIREO. **166–177** Brian E. Small. **178** Mark W. Lockwood. **179–182** Brian E. Small. **183** Alan Murphy. **184** Brian E. Small. **185** Brian E. Small (L), Alan Murphy (R). **186** Brian E. Small (T), Alan Murphy (B). **187** Brian E. Small. **188** Brian E. Small (T), Alan Murphy (B). **189–201** Brian E. Small. **202** Alan Murphy. **203–206** Brian E. Small **207** Brian E. Small (T), Rick Bowers (B). **208–231** Brian E. Small. **232** Mark W. Lockwood. **233–242** Brian E. Small. **243** Brian E. Small (T), Bob Steele (B). **244** Brian E. Small. **245** Brian E. Small (T), Greg Lasley (B). **246–296** Brian E. Small. **297** Alan Murphy. **298–303** Brian E. Small. **304** Alan Murphy. **305–307** Brian E. Small.

Chcklist of the Birds of Texas

This list includes all birds that have been documented in Texas as of 2020. The official state list is maintained by the Texas Bird Records Committee (TBRC) which is a standing committee of the Texas Ornithological Society. Common names, taxonomy and sequence follow the *American Ornithologists' Union's (AOU) Check-list of North American Birds*. The TBRC requests documentation that would include a written description, and when possible photographs, for all of these species. There are two extinct birds (E) on this list, Passenger Pigeon and Carolina Parakeet, and two others that are very likely extinct, Eskimo Curlew and Ivory-billed Woodpecker.

Family Anatidae: Ducks, Geese, and Waterfowl

- ☐ Black-bellied Whistling-Duck
- ☐ Fulvous Whistling-Duck
- ☐ Snow Goose
- ☐ Ross's Goose
- ☐ Greater White-fronted Goose
- ☐ Brant
- ☐ Cackling Goose
- ☐ Canada Goose
- ☐ Trumpeter Swan
- ☐ Tundra Swan
- ☐ Muscovy Duck
- ☐ Wood Duck
- ☐ Garganey
- ☐ Blue-winged Teal
- ☐ Cinnamon Teal
- ☐ Northern Shoveler
- ☐ Gadwall
- ☐ Eurasian Wigeon
- ☐ American Wigeon
- ☐ Mallard
- ☐ Mexican Duck
- ☐ American Black Duck
- ☐ Mottled Duck
- ☐ White-cheeked Pintail
- ☐ Northern Pintail
- ☐ Green-winged Teal
- ☐ Canvasback
- ☐ Redhead
- ☐ Ring-necked Duck
- ☐ Greater Scaup
- ☐ Lesser Scaup
- ☐ King Eider
- ☐ Common Eider
- ☐ Harlequin Duck
- ☐ Surf Scoter
- ☐ White-winged Scoter
- ☐ Black Scoter
- ☐ Long-tailed Duck
- ☐ Bufflehead
- ☐ Common Goldeneye
- ☐ Barrow's Goldeneye
- ☐ Hooded Merganser
- ☐ Common Merganser
- ☐ Red-breasted Merganser
- ☐ Masked Duck
- ☐ Ruddy Duck

Family Cracidae: Guans

- ☐ Plain Chachalaca

Family Odontophoridae: New World Quail

- ☐ Northern Bobwhite
- ☐ Scaled Quail
- ☐ Gambel's Quail
- ☐ Montezuma Quail

Family Phasianidae: Pheasants, Grouse, and Turkeys

- ☐ Wild Turkey
- ☐ Greater Prairie-Chicken
- ☐ Lesser Prairie-Chicken
- ☐ Ring-necked Pheasant

Family Phoenicopteridae: Flamingos

- ☐ American Flamingo

Family Podicipedidae: Grebes

- ☐ Least Grebe
- ☐ Pied-billed Grebe
- ☐ Horned Grebe
- ☐ Red-necked Grebe
- ☐ Eared Grebe
- ☐ Western Grebe
- ☐ Clark's Grebe

Family Columbidae: Pigeons and Doves

- ☐ Rock Pigeon
- ☐ White-crowned Pigeon
- ☐ Red-billed Pigeon
- ☐ Band-tailed Pigeon
- ☐ Eurasian Collared-Dove
- ☐ Passenger Pigeon E
- ☐ Inca Dove
- ☐ Common Ground Dove

- ☐ Ruddy Ground Dove
- ☐ Ruddy Quail-Dove
- ☐ White-tipped Dove
- ☐ White-winged Dove
- ☐ Mourning Dove

Family Cuculidae: Cuckoos

- ☐ Groove-billed Ani
- ☐ Greater Roadrunner
- ☐ Dark-billed Cuckoo
- ☐ Yellow-billed Cuckoo
- ☐ Mangrove Cuckoo
- ☐ Black-billed Cuckoo

Family Caprimulgidae: Nightjars

- ☐ Lesser Nighthawk
- ☐ Common Nighthawk
- ☐ Common Pauraque
- ☐ Common Poorwill
- ☐ Chuck-will's-widow
- ☐ Eastern Whip-poor-will
- ☐ Mexican Whip-poor-will

Family Apodidae: Swifts

- ☐ Black Swift
- ☐ White-collared Swift
- ☐ Chimney Swift
- ☐ White-throated Swift

Family Trochilidae: Hummingbirds

- ☐ Mexican Violetear
- ☐ Green-breasted Mango
- ☐ Rivoli's Hummingbird
- ☐ Amethyst-throated Mountain-gem
- ☐ Blue-throated Mountain-gem
- ☐ Lucifer Hummingbird
- ☐ Ruby-throated Hummingbird
- ☐ Black-chinned Hummingbird
- ☐ Anna's Hummingbird
- ☐ Costa's Hummingbird
- ☐ Calliope Hummingbird
- ☐ Rufous Hummingbird
- ☐ Allen's Hummingbird
- ☐ Broad-tailed Hummingbird
- ☐ Broad-billed Hummingbird
- ☐ White-eared Hummingbird
- ☐ Violet-crowned Hummingbird
- ☐ Berylline Hummingbird
- ☐ Buff-bellied Hummingbird

Family Rallidae: Rails and Coots

- ☐ Paint-billed Crake
- ☐ Spotted Rail
- ☐ Clapper Rail
- ☐ King Rail
- ☐ Virginia Rail
- ☐ Sora
- ☐ Common Gallinule
- ☐ American Coot
- ☐ Purple Gallinule
- ☐ Yellow Rail
- ☐ Black Rail

Family Gruidae: Cranes

- ☐ Sandhill Crane
- ☐ Common Crane
- ☐ Whooping Crane

Family Burhinidae: Thick-knees

- ☐ Double-striped Thick-knee

Family Recurvirostridae: Stilts and Avocets

- ☐ Black-necked Stilt
- ☐ American Avocet

Family Haematopodidae: Oystercatchers

- ☐ American Oystercatcher

Family Charadriidae: Plovers

- ☐ Black-bellied Plover
- ☐ American Golden-Plover
- ☐ Pacific Golden-Plover
- ☐ Killdeer
- ☐ Semipalmated Plover
- ☐ Piping Plover
- ☐ Wilson's Plover
- ☐ Collared Plover
- ☐ Mountain Plover
- ☐ Snowy Plover

Family Jacanidae: Jacanas

- ☐ Northern Jacana

Family Scolopacidae: Sandpipers

- ☐ Upland Sandpiper
- ☐ Whimbrel
- ☐ Eskimo Curlew
- ☐ Long-billed Curlew
- ☐ Bar-tailed Godwit
- ☐ Black-tailed Godwit
- ☐ Hudsonian Godwit
- ☐ Marbled Godwit
- ☐ Ruddy Turnstone
- ☐ Black Turnstone
- ☐ Red Knot
- ☐ Surfbird
- ☐ Ruff
- ☐ Sharp-tailed Sandpiper
- ☐ Stilt Sandpiper
- ☐ Curlew Sandpiper
- ☐ Red-necked Stint
- ☐ Sanderling
- ☐ Dunlin
- ☐ Purple Sandpiper
- ☐ Baird's Sandpiper
- ☐ Least Sandpiper
- ☐ White-rumped Sandpiper
- ☐ Buff-breasted Sandpiper
- ☐ Pectoral Sandpiper
- ☐ Semipalmated Sandpiper
- ☐ Western Sandpiper
- ☐ Short-billed Dowitcher
- ☐ Long-billed Dowitcher
- ☐ American Woodcock
- ☐ Wilson's Snipe
- ☐ Spotted Sandpiper
- ☐ Solitary Sandpiper
- ☐ Wandering Tattler
- ☐ Lesser Yellowlegs
- ☐ Willet
- ☐ Spotted Redshank
- ☐ Greater Yellowlegs
- ☐ Wilson's Phalarope
- ☐ Red-necked Phalarope
- ☐ Red Phalarope

Family Stercorariidae: Skuas and Jaegers

- ☐ South Polar Skua
- ☐ Pomarine Jaeger
- ☐ Parasitic Jaeger
- ☐ Long-tailed Jaeger

Family Laridae: Gulls, Terns, and Skimmers

- ☐ Black-legged Kittiwake
- ☐ Sabine's Gull
- ☐ Bonaparte's Gull
- ☐ Black-headed Gull
- ☐ Little Gull
- ☐ Laughing Gull
- ☐ Franklin's Gull
- ☐ Black-tailed Gull
- ☐ Heermann's Gull
- ☐ Mew Gull
- ☐ Ring-billed Gull
- ☐ Western Gull
- ☐ California Gull
- ☐ Herring Gull
- ☐ Yellow-legged Gull
- ☐ Iceland Gull
- ☐ Lesser Black-backed Gull
- ☐ Slaty-backed Gull
- ☐ Glaucous-winged Gull
- ☐ Glaucous Gull
- ☐ Great Black-backed Gull
- ☐ Kelp Gull
- ☐ Brown Noddy
- ☐ Black Noddy
- ☐ Sooty Tern
- ☐ Bridled Tern
- ☐ Least Tern
- ☐ Gull-billed Tern
- ☐ Caspian Tern
- ☐ Black Tern
- ☐ Roseate Tern
- ☐ Common Tern
- ☐ Arctic Tern
- ☐ Forster's Tern
- ☐ Royal Tern
- ☐ Sandwich Tern
- ☐ Elegant Tern
- ☐ Black Skimmer

Family Phaethontidae: Tropicbirds

- ☐ White-tailed Tropicbird
- ☐ Red-billed Tropicbird

Family Gaviidae: Loons

- ☐ Red-throated Loon
- ☐ Pacific Loon
- ☐ Common Loon
- ☐ Yellow-billed Loon

Family Diomedeidae: Albatrosses

- ☐ Yellow-nosed Albatross

Family Oceanitidae: Southern Storm-Petrels

- ☐ Wilson's Storm-Petrel

Family Hydrobatidae: Northern Storm-Petrels

- ☐ Leach's Storm-Petrel
- ☐ Band-rumped Storm-Petrel

Family Procellariidae: Shearwaters and Petrels

- ☐ Black-capped Petrel
- ☐ Stejneger's Petrel
- ☐ White-chinned Petrel
- ☐ Cory's Shearwater
- ☐ Sooty Shearwater
- ☐ Great Shearwater
- ☐ Manx Shearwater
- ☐ Audubon's Shearwater

Family Ciconiidae: Storks

- ☐ Jabiru
- ☐ Wood Stork

Family Fregatidae: Frigatebirds

- ☐ Magnificent Frigatebird

Family Sulidae: Boobies and Gannets

- ☐ Masked Booby
- ☐ Blue-footed Booby
- ☐ Brown Booby
- ☐ Red-footed Booby
- ☐ Northern Gannet

Family Anhingidae: Anhingas

- ☐ Anhinga

Family Phalacrocoracidae: Cormorants

- ☐ Double-crested Cormorant
- ☐ Neotropic Cormorant

Family Pelecanidae: Pelicans

- ☐ American White Pelican
- ☐ Brown Pelican

Family Ardeidae: Bitterns and Herons

- ☐ American Bittern
- ☐ Least Bittern
- ☐ Bare-throated Tiger-Heron
- ☐ Great Blue Heron
- ☐ Great Egret
- ☐ Snowy Egret
- ☐ Little Blue Heron
- ☐ Tricolored Heron
- ☐ Reddish Egret
- ☐ Cattle Egret
- ☐ Green Heron
- ☐ Black-crowned Night-Heron
- ☐ Yellow-crowned Night-Heron

Family Threskiornithidae: Ibises and Spoonbills

- ☐ White Ibis
- ☐ Glossy Ibis
- ☐ White-faced Ibis
- ☐ Roseate Spoonbill

Family Cathartidae: New World Vultures

- ☐ Black Vulture
- ☐ Turkey Vulture

Family Pandionidae: Osprey

- ☐ Osprey

Family Accipitridae: Hawks, Eagles, and Kites

- ☐ White-tailed Kite
- ☐ Hook-billed Kite
- ☐ Swallow-tailed Kite
- ☐ Golden Eagle
- ☐ Double-toothed Kite
- ☐ Northern Harrier
- ☐ Sharp-shinned Hawk
- ☐ Cooper's Hawk
- ☐ Northern Goshawk
- ☐ Bald Eagle
- ☐ Mississippi Kite
- ☐ Crane Hawk
- ☐ Snail Kite
- ☐ Common Black Hawk
- ☐ Great Black Hawk
- ☐ Roadside Hawk
- ☐ Harris's Hawk
- ☐ White-tailed Hawk
- ☐ Gray Hawk
- ☐ Red-shouldered Hawk
- ☐ Broad-winged Hawk

- ☐ Short-tailed Hawk
- ☐ Swainson's Hawk
- ☐ Zone-tailed Hawk
- ☐ Red-tailed Hawk
- ☐ Rough-legged Hawk
- ☐ Ferruginous Hawk

Family Tytonidae: Barn Owls

- ☐ Barn Owl

Family Strigidae: Owls

- ☐ Flammulated Owl
- ☐ Western Screech-Owl
- ☐ Eastern Screech-Owl
- ☐ Great Horned Owl
- ☐ Snowy Owl
- ☐ Northern Pygmy-Owl
- ☐ Ferruginous Pygmy-Owl
- ☐ Elf Owl
- ☐ Burrowing Owl
- ☐ Mottled Owl
- ☐ Spotted Owl
- ☐ Barred Owl
- ☐ Long-eared Owl
- ☐ Stygian Owl
- ☐ Short-eared Owl
- ☐ Northern Saw-whet Owl

Family Trogonidae: Trogons

- ☐ Elegant Trogon

Family Alcedinidae: Kingfishers

- ☐ Ringed Kingfisher
- ☐ Belted Kingfisher
- ☐ Amazon Kingfisher
- ☐ Green Kingfisher

Family Picidae: Woodpeckers

- ☐ Lewis's Woodpecker
- ☐ Red-headed Woodpecker
- ☐ Acorn Woodpecker
- ☐ Golden-fronted Woodpecker
- ☐ Red-bellied Woodpecker
- ☐ Williamson's Sapsucker
- ☐ Yellow-bellied Sapsucker
- ☐ Red-naped Sapsucker
- ☐ Red-breasted Sapsucker
- ☐ Downy Woodpecker
- ☐ Ladder-backed Woodpecker
- ☐ Red-cockaded Woodpecker
- ☐ Hairy Woodpecker
- ☐ Northern Flicker
- ☐ Pileated Woodpecker
- ☐ Ivory-billed Woodpecker [E]

Family Falconidae: Falcons and Caracaras

- ☐ Collared Forest-Falcon
- ☐ Crested Caracara
- ☐ American Kestrel
- ☐ Merlin
- ☐ Aplomado Falcon
- ☐ Gyrfalcon
- ☐ Peregrine Falcon
- ☐ Prairie Falcon

Family Psittacidae: Parrots

- ☐ Monk Parakeet [E]
- ☐ Carolina Parakeet
- ☐ Green Parakeet
- ☐ Red-crowned Parrot

Family Thamnophilidae: Antshrikes and Antbirds

- ☐ Barred Antshrike

Family Tityridae: Tityras, Becards, and allies

- ☐ Masked Tityra
- ☐ Rose-throated Becard

Family Tyrannidae: Tyrant Flycatchers

- ☐ Northern Beardless-Tyrannulet
- ☐ Greenish Elaenia
- ☐ White-crested Elaenia
- ☐ Dusky-capped Flycatcher
- ☐ Ash-throated Flycatcher
- ☐ Nutting's Flycatcher
- ☐ Great Crested Flycatcher
- ☐ Brown-crested Flycatcher
- ☐ Great Kiskadee
- ☐ Social Flycatcher
- ☐ Sulphur-bellied Flycatcher
- ☐ Piratic Flycatcher
- ☐ Variegated Flycatcher
- ☐ Tropical Kingbird
- ☐ Couch's Kingbird
- ☐ Cassin's Kingbird
- ☐ Thick-billed Kingbird
- ☐ Western Kingbird
- ☐ Eastern Kingbird
- ☐ Gray Kingbird
- ☐ Scissor-tailed Flycatcher
- ☐ Fork-tailed Flycatcher
- ☐ Tufted Flycatcher
- ☐ Olive-sided Flycatcher
- ☐ Greater Pewee
- ☐ Western Wood-Pewee
- ☐ Eastern Wood-Pewee
- ☐ Yellow-bellied Flycatcher
- ☐ Acadian Flycatcher
- ☐ Alder Flycatcher
- ☐ Willow Flycatcher
- ☐ Least Flycatcher
- ☐ Hammond's Flycatcher
- ☐ Gray Flycatcher
- ☐ Dusky Flycatcher
- ☐ Pacific-slope Flycatcher
- ☐ Cordilleran Flycatcher
- ☐ Buff-breasted Flycatcher
- ☐ Black Phoebe
- ☐ Eastern Phoebe
- ☐ Say's Phoebe
- ☐ Vermilion Flycatcher

Family Laniidae: Shrikes

- ☐ Loggerhead Shrike
- ☐ Northern Shrike

Family Vireonidae: Vireos

- ☐ Black-capped Vireo
- ☐ White-eyed Vireo
- ☐ Bell's Vireo
- ☐ Gray Vireo
- ☐ Hutton's Vireo
- ☐ Yellow-throated Vireo
- ☐ Cassin's Vireo
- ☐ Blue-headed Vireo
- ☐ Plumbeous Vireo
- ☐ Philadelphia Vireo
- ☐ Warbling Vireo
- ☐ Red-eyed Vireo
- ☐ Yellow-green Vireo
- ☐ Black-whiskered Vireo
- ☐ Yucatan Vireo

Family Corvidae: Crows, Jays, and Magpies

- ☐ Brown Jay
- ☐ Green Jay
- ☐ Pinyon Jay
- ☐ Steller's Jay
- ☐ Blue Jay
- ☐ Woodhouse's Scrub-Jay

- ☐ Mexican Jay
- ☐ Clark's Nutcracker
- ☐ Black-billed Magpie
- ☐ American Crow
- ☐ Tamaulipas Crow
- ☐ Fish Crow
- ☐ Chihuahuan Raven
- ☐ Common Raven

Family Alaudidae: Larks

- ☐ Horned Lark

Family Hirundinidae: Swallows

- ☐ Bank Swallow
- ☐ Tree Swallow
- ☐ Violet-green Swallow
- ☐ Northern Rough-winged Swallow
- ☐ Purple Martin
- ☐ Gray-breasted Martin
- ☐ Barn Swallow
- ☐ Cliff Swallow
- ☐ Cave Swallow

Family Paridae: Chickadees, and Titmice

- ☐ Carolina Chickadee
- ☐ Black-capped Chickadee
- ☐ Mountain Chickadee
- ☐ Juniper Titmouse
- ☐ Tufted Titmouse
- ☐ Black-crested Titmouse

Family Remizidae: Penduline-Tits

- ☐ Verdin

Family Aegithalidae: Long-tailed Tits

- ☐ Bushtit

Family Sittidae: Nuthatches

- ☐ Red-breasted Nuthatch
- ☐ White-breasted Nuthatch
- ☐ Pygmy Nuthatch
- ☐ Brown-headed Nuthatch

Family Certhiidae: Treecreepers

- ☐ Brown Creeper

Family Troglodytidae: Wrens

- ☐ Rock Wren
- ☐ Canyon Wren
- ☐ House Wren
- ☐ Winter Wren
- ☐ Sedge Wren
- ☐ Marsh Wren
- ☐ Carolina Wren
- ☐ Bewick's Wren
- ☐ Cactus Wren

Family Polioptilidae: Gnatcatchers

- ☐ Blue-gray Gnatcatcher
- ☐ Black-tailed Gnatcatcher

Family Cinclidae: Dippers

- ☐ American Dipper

Family Regulidae: Kinglets

- ☐ Golden-crowned Kinglet
- ☐ Ruby-crowned Kinglet

Family Muscicapidae: Old World Flycatchers

- ☐ Northern Wheatear

Family Turdidae: Thrushes

- ☐ Eastern Bluebird
- ☐ Western Bluebird
- ☐ Mountain Bluebird
- ☐ Townsend's Solitaire
- ☐ Orange-billed Nightingale-Thrush
- ☐ Black-headed Nightingale-Thrush
- ☐ Veery
- ☐ Gray-cheeked Thrush
- ☐ Swainson's Thrush
- ☐ Hermit Thrush
- ☐ Wood Thrush
- ☐ Clay-colored Thrush
- ☐ White-throated Thrush
- ☐ Rufous-backed Robin
- ☐ American Robin
- ☐ Varied Thrush
- ☐ Aztec Thrush

Family Mimidae: Mockingbirds and Thrashers

- ☐ Blue Mockingbird
- ☐ Black Catbird
- ☐ Gray Catbird
- ☐ Curve-billed Thrasher
- ☐ Brown Thrasher
- ☐ Long-billed Thrasher
- ☐ Crissal Thrasher
- ☐ Sage Thrasher
- ☐ Northern Mockingbird

Family Sturnidae: Starlings

- ☐ European Starling

Family Bombycillidae: Waxwings

- ☐ Bohemian Waxwing
- ☐ Cedar Waxwing

Family Ptiliogonatidae: Silky-flycatchers

- ☐ Gray Silky-flycatcher
- ☐ Phainopepla

Family Peucedramidae: Olive Warbler

- ☐ Olive Warbler

Family Passeridae: Old World Sparrows

- ☐ House Sparrow

Family Motacillidae: Wagtails and Pipits

- ☐ White Wagtail
- ☐ American Pipit
- ☐ Sprague's Pipit

Family Fringillidae: Finches

- ☐ Evening Grosbeak
- ☐ Pine Grosbeak
- ☐ Gray-crowned Rosy-Finch
- ☐ House Finch
- ☐ Purple Finch
- ☐ Cassin's Finch
- ☐ Common Redpoll
- ☐ Red Crossbill
- ☐ White-winged Crossbill
- ☐ Pine Siskin
- ☐ Lesser Goldfinch
- ☐ Lawrence's Goldfinch
- ☐ American Goldfinch

Family Calcariidae: Longspurs and Snow Buntings

- ☐ Lapland Longspur
- ☐ Chestnut-collared Longspur
- ☐ Smith's Longspur
- ☐ Thick-billed Longspur
- ☐ Snow Bunting

Family Passerellidae: New World Sparrows

- ☐ Botteri's Sparrow
- ☐ Cassin's Sparrow
- ☐ Bachman's Sparrow
- ☐ Grasshopper Sparrow
- ☐ Olive Sparrow
- ☐ Black-throated Sparrow
- ☐ Lark Sparrow
- ☐ Lark Bunting
- ☐ Chipping Sparrow
- ☐ Clay-colored Sparrow
- ☐ Black-chinned Sparrow
- ☐ Field Sparrow
- ☐ Brewer's Sparrow
- ☐ Fox Sparrow
- ☐ American Tree Sparrow
- ☐ Dark-eyed Junco
- ☐ Yellow-eyed Junco
- ☐ White-crowned Sparrow
- ☐ Golden-crowned Sparrow
- ☐ Harris's Sparrow
- ☐ White-throated Sparrow
- ☐ Sagebrush Sparrow
- ☐ Vesper Sparrow
- ☐ LeConte's Sparrow
- ☐ Seaside Sparrow
- ☐ Nelson's Sparrow
- ☐ Baird's Sparrow
- ☐ Henslow's Sparrow
- ☐ Savannah Sparrow
- ☐ Song Sparrow
- ☐ Lincoln's Sparrow
- ☐ Swamp Sparrow
- ☐ Canyon Towhee
- ☐ Rufous-crowned Sparrow
- ☐ Green-tailed Towhee
- ☐ Spotted Towhee
- ☐ Eastern Towhee

Family Icteriidae: Yellow-breasted Chat

- ☐ Yellow-breasted Chat

Family Icteridae: Blackbirds

- ☐ Yellow-headed Blackbird
- ☐ Bobolink
- ☐ Eastern Meadowlark
- ☐ Western Meadowlark
- ☐ Black-vented Oriole
- ☐ Orchard Oriole
- ☐ Hooded Oriole
- ☐ Streak-backed Oriole
- ☐ Bullock's Oriole
- ☐ Altamira Oriole
- ☐ Audubon's Oriole
- ☐ Baltimore Oriole
- ☐ Scott's Oriole
- ☐ Red-winged Blackbird
- ☐ Shiny Cowbird
- ☐ Bronzed Cowbird
- ☐ Brown-headed Cowbird
- ☐ Rusty Blackbird
- ☐ Brewer's Blackbird
- ☐ Common Grackle
- ☐ Boat-tailed Grackle
- ☐ Great-tailed Grackle

Family Parulidae: New World Warblers

- ☐ Ovenbird
- ☐ Worm-eating Warbler
- ☐ Louisiana Waterthrush
- ☐ Northern Waterthrush
- ☐ Golden-winged Warbler
- ☐ Blue-winged Warbler
- ☐ Black-and-white Warbler
- ☐ Prothonotary Warbler
- ☐ Swainson's Warbler
- ☐ Tennessee Warbler
- ☐ Orange-crowned Warbler
- ☐ Colima Warbler
- ☐ Lucy's Warbler
- ☐ Nashville Warbler
- ☐ Virginia's Warbler
- ☐ Connecticut Warbler
- ☐ Gray-crowned Yellowthroat
- ☐ MacGillivray's Warbler
- ☐ Mourning Warbler
- ☐ Kentucky Warbler
- ☐ Common Yellowthroat
- ☐ Hooded Warbler
- ☐ American Redstart
- ☐ Cape May Warbler
- ☐ Cerulean Warbler
- ☐ Northern Parula
- ☐ Tropical Parula
- ☐ Magnolia Warbler
- ☐ Bay-breasted Warbler
- ☐ Blackburnian Warbler
- ☐ Yellow Warbler
- ☐ Chestnut-sided Warbler
- ☐ Blackpoll Warbler
- ☐ Black-throated Blue Warbler
- ☐ Palm Warbler
- ☐ Pine Warbler
- ☐ Yellow-rumped Warbler
- ☐ Yellow-throated Warbler
- ☐ Prairie Warbler
- ☐ Grace's Warbler
- ☐ Black-throated Gray Warbler
- ☐ Townsend's Warbler
- ☐ Hermit Warbler
- ☐ Golden-cheeked Warbler
- ☐ Black-throated Green Warbler
- ☐ Fan-tailed Warbler
- ☐ Rufous-capped Warbler
- ☐ Golden-crowned Warbler
- ☐ Canada Warbler
- ☐ Wilson's Warbler
- ☐ Red-faced Warbler
- ☐ Painted Redstart
- ☐ Slate-throated Redstart

Family Cardinalidae: Cardinals and Allies

- ☐ Hepatic Tanager
- ☐ Summer Tanager
- ☐ Scarlet Tanager
- ☐ Western Tanager
- ☐ Flame-colored Tanager
- ☐ Crimson-collared Grosbeak
- ☐ Northern Cardinal
- ☐ Pyrrhuloxia
- ☐ Yellow Grosbeak
- ☐ Rose-breasted Grosbeak
- ☐ Black-headed Grosbeak
- ☐ Blue Bunting
- ☐ Blue Grosbeak
- ☐ Lazuli Bunting
- ☐ Indigo Bunting
- ☐ Varied Bunting
- ☐ Painted Bunting
- ☐ Dickcissel

Family Thraupidae: Tanagers and Allies

- ☐ Red-legged Honeycreeper
- ☐ Yellow-faced Grassquit
- ☐ Morelet's Seedeater

Species Index

T

V

W

Y

Z

Mark W. Lockwood recently retired as a conservation biologist with the Texas Parks and Wildlife Department. He was awarded the Ludlow Griscom Award for Outstanding Contributions in Regional Ornithology from the American Birding Association in 2012. He is a member of the Texas Bird Records Committee and the American Birding Association's Checklist Committee and is the author of eight books including *The TOS Handbook of Texas Birds* (Texas A&M Press). He lives in Alpine, Texas.

Brian E. Small is a full-time professional bird and nature photographer. For more than 25 years, he has traveled widely across North America to capture images of birds in their native habitats. He served as the photo editor for *Birding* magazine for 15 years. Small grew up in Los Angeles, graduated from U.C.L.A. in 1982, and still lives there today with his wife Ana, daughter Nicole, and son Tyler.

THE ABA STATE FIELD GUIDE SERIES

ARIZONA
ISBN 978-1-935622-60-4

CALIFORNIA
ISBN 978-1-935622-50-5

CAROLINAS
ISBN 978-1-935622-63-5

COLORADO
ISBN 978-1-935622-43-7

FLORIDA
ISBN 978-1-935622-48-2

HAWAI'I
ISBN 978-1-935622-71-0

ILLINOIS
ISBN 978-1-935622-62-8

MASSACHUSETTS
ISBN 978-1-935622-66-6

MICHIGAN
ISBN 978-1-935622-67-3

MINNESOTA
ISBN 978-1-935622-59-8

NEW JERSEY
ISBN 978-1-935622-42-0

NEW YORK
ISBN 978-1-935622-51-2

OHIO
ISBN 978-1-935622-70-3

OREGON
ISBN 978-1-935622-68-0

PENNSYLVANIA
ISBN 978-1-935622-52-9

TEXAS
ISBN 978-1-935622-53-6

WASHINGTON
ISBN 978-1-935622-72-7

WISCONSIN
ISBN 978-1-935622-69-7